TRUE STORY

FEAR NOT

for I am with you

By
JEFF YOSICK and JIM YOSICK

Other Books by Jeff Yosick - Children's Stories:

Timmy and the Storm
When Daddy Comes Home
Bryanna and the Sand
Snowflakes from Heaven
Running the Race
One Penny One Hope
Madison's Special Dolly

Copyright

Narrow Path Publications

www.narrowpathbooks.com

Scripture taken from THE HOLY BIBLE, NEW INTERNATIONAL VERSION*
Copyright 1973, 1978, 1984 by International Bible Society.
Used by permission of Zondervan Publishing House. All right reserved.

Cover Design and layout by Phyllis Stewart
Phyllis can be contacted at pstewart0831@sbcglobal.net

Printed in the USA

Dedication

Thank you, Jeff, for taking this to the next level. Only by the guiding of the Holy Spirit could this book have been written.

Thank you, Barb, for all that you've given me, especially your love and hope.

To my children and their spouses, Jeff and Valerie, Angie and Jeff, Todd and Amy, and Jenny and Craig for all your support and love.

To my eight grandchildren, Brooke, Courtney, Tori, Bryanna, Brock, Alivia, Brenner and Logan for all your artwork, hugs and kisses.

Lastly, to all those who have prayed for me. It was by your faith I was healed.

A special thank you to the nurses and doctors who cared for me at OSU James Cancer Center. May God bless you all.

-Jim

I want to thank and dedicate this book to my father. I'll never be able to put into words what an inspiration you've been to me. I've learned many wonderful lessons from you through the years, but nothing compared to those difficult and jubilant days during 2008. Your faith in God is incredible and I'm proud to be your son. I'd also like to thank my Heavenly Father for the inspiration and gentle nudges throughout this process.

-Jeff

Table of Contents

Foreword

There were many different ways I could have approached this book and subject matter. In fact, the events were something I needed to mentally work through before beginning to put words onto paper. I've spent many days over the past year dodging thoughts and unseen nudges, but I simply couldn't run any longer. God kept my father here for a reason, He wanted this story to be told.

I've always considered myself a children's author. Everything I've ever put into book form has been for children. Although my stories are intended for younger eyes, I carry a mission to incorporate a life lesson within each book. Life lessons for the entire audience reading the book young, and old.

The pages between the covers of this book also contain a life lesson. You'll be taken on a journey to what I hope will result in a closer relationship with those near and dear to you, but more importantly a closer relationship with God. It's my sincere prayer it will provide an opportunity for you to experience God in a new way and witness firsthand the mercy and grace He provides for all of us.

The journey my father endured in 2008 has had a profound effect on our entire family. Writing this book has helped me to realize I serve a living God who loves me very much. I've come to know the importance of daily worship and communion with God through His word. I've sensed my relationship with God become more personal and powerful than ever before.

My time spent on this project has brought me to a new horizon in writing. It's provided me the opportunity to share some pieces of my life while continually pointing to the fact that nothing in this world happens by chance. There is a God who watches over us. He is ever gracious, and He loves us unconditionally.

I feel honored to have co-authored this book with my father. When I first approached him with the idea of putting a book together about his battle with cancer he was excited and ready to go. No words will ever be able to express the inspiration he's been for me. It was a pure joy to collaborate with him on such a powerful story. I will cherish all of the wonderful and tough moments throughout my life with him, especially the miraculous journey he and my entire family shared in 2008.

-Jeff

Preface

I don't consider myself a writer or public speaker by any means. The opportunity to be a part of this book has allowed me to share my special testimony. I have many of them, but this is one I pray will impact your life forever, as it has mine.

The following pages contain the story about my battle with a frightening disease called renal (kidney) cancer, and how God spoke to me and my family through our struggles with it. In writing my pieces of the book I've had some trouble at times remembering some of the events which took place. My family has done a good job of helping me to fill in those moments that remain at times a bit fuzzy to me.

What I went through a year ago is a drop in the bucket compared to what other people endure in their lives. There are literally millions of people who suffer from ailments each and every day. These people suffer for years just grasping for a hope things will one day get better.

Folks, it's very important we pray for one another, especially for those who are suffering. We need to be there to offer encouragement and do all we can to lighten their burdens. We must take hold of the belief that through our encouragement and prayer those suffering will be able to find the hope available in Christ through these trials. This doesn't mean the problems or sickness will always disappear, but the knowledge of having groups of people praying for you can often be more important than medicine.

It's my sincere hope this story and testimony will encourage and inspire you. I pray the book will speak to you in such a way that it will change your life forever.

-Jim

CHAPTER

1

My Journey Begins

Chapter 1
My Journey Begins

Before I begin, I'd like to tell you a little bit about myself. I was born the second child of eight to a couple of hardworking parents. My father was a bricklayer and my mother was a homemaker. I grew up in the small town of New Washington, Ohio. It's a quaint small Midwestern town with a population that would be close to Mayberry.

I married my high school sweetheart Barbara Snipes and God blessed us with 4 wonderful caring children, 2 boys, and 2 girls, Jeff, Angie, Todd, and Jenny. They are all married to the best daughters and sons-in-law a person could ever hope for. Together they've brought into our lives 8 beautiful grandchildren, 5 girls, and 3 boys.

We've always been a very close knit family. Although there is some distance between us, our family gatherings come around often and are a pure joy for all of us. We love to celebrate all of the birthdays and holidays together. Each one of them presents another chance for us to be together.

I was employed as a machine repairman at the Timken Company in Bucyrus, Ohio, for 36 years. I've been retired for awhile now and have enjoyed it very much. Barb has also retired. She was employed as a nurse for 23 years at Heartland Nursing Home in Bucyrus.

The journey that led to the writing of this book began toward the end of January in 2008. I'd suffered what was thought to be a mild heart attack. I was transported to a hospital located in Mansfield, Ohio, where labs were drawn and an EKG was completed. It was then decided by my cardiologist for me to have a heart catheterization. The procedure showed no blockages or damage, and other than a few months of cardiac rehabilitation no further treatment was required.

My time in rehab through February and March went very well. I had very little difficulty with the workout regime prescribed to me. I found myself actually getting into pretty good shape and felt good.

The next couple of months were a different story. In April I'd developed a low grade fever accompanied with extreme fatigue. It lasted about a week and I eventually felt much better.

In May this strange fever and fatigue struck again. It lasted longer this time but was treated as nothing more than a recurring virus. The fever eventually dissipated, but the waves of fatigue continued. Things just didn't feel right.

-Jim

It was a typical cold Ohio morning in late January when I received the call from my sister Angie. Judging by the concern in her voice I knew something serious was happening, and it wasn't long before she proceeded to tell me our father was being transported to a hospital in Mansfield, Ohio. From all indications there was a problem with his heart. I immediately dropped all I was doing, explained things to my fellow associates at work, and headed for Mansfield.

My place of employment is toward the north end of Columbus, Ohio. The drive to Mansfield from that location normally takes about an hour. That day, however, was different. My overwhelming fear and anxiety over what was happening had translated into a little extra pressure on the gas pedal. This resulted in a significant reduction of drive time and a quicker time of arrival.

When I entered the emergency room waiting area I was greeted by my younger sister Jennifer. There was a look of worry and concern etched across her face. After a quick hug she updated me on everything before walking me back to where our father was being treated.

I am employed in the field of healthcare. Through my 20 years of experience I'd grown accustomed to the sights, sounds, and smells, of medical environments. However, none of my training or experience had ever prepared me for seeing my own father in an emergency room.

I gave him a big hug when I first saw him, and soon noticed he was in good spirits and full of his typical humor. My father had been blessed with the knack for a quick joke or remark that could lighten up any room regardless the situation. This day was no different. He was up to his usual antics with all of us, including the medical staff caring for him. He had something to say about everything, from the heart monitor wiring, to the gown he was wearing, there was something funny to say.

After a short wait, a cardiologist entered the room with results of my father's EKG and blood work that were done upon his arrival. The blood work was all normal, and the EKG showed a slight change from one previously performed a few weeks earlier. To verify there were no active blockages, the cardiologist suggested he should have a heart catheterization procedure.

When it was time for my father to be transported for the catheterization we were shown to a different waiting area. We were the only family there at the time and it was very quiet. My thoughts wandered off to the many people that had also sat in that very room experiencing the same thoughts and fears. There were probably several families there that very same day.

My mother, two sisters and I paged through different magazines as we awaited word from the doctor. There was some discussion about the procedure and what the results might be, but a lot of time was also spent reassuring each other that everything would turn out fine.

An hour had passed by before we'd received word from the doctor. The news was very good for all of us. There were no significant blockages found in his heart and no sign of any damage. My father would be admitted for a couple of days to monitor things, but other than some cardiac rehabilitation and medication adjustments he'd be just fine.

Over the next couple of months my father followed the cardiologist's instructions and took part in cardiac rehabilitation. He also made a pointed effort to follow a stricter diet by watching his caloric intake each day. He kept away from sweets and became better friends with fruits and vegetables. His dedication to this change in diet brought along the benefit of shedding a few pounds.

The cooler air of March soon faded and April rolled in with the promise of spring. After waging through another long Ohio winter it was good to feel the warmer air once again. It was on one of those first days in April that I'd given my father a call. He mentioned he'd been ill from a flu bug or virus. He was running a slight fever and felt run down. I agreed the symptoms were that of a flu or virus and told him it'd probably be gone after a few days.

The rest of April seemed to go very well for my father, but in May he experienced another unexpected onset of the fatigue and fever. The initial assessment by his physician was a recurrence of the virus from April, but this time a series of blood tests were performed. They came back normal and within a week his symptoms had once again subsided. Before long he'd returned back to his normal routine but suffered from intermittent waves of fatigue.

Moments with God

"Consider it pure joy, my brothers, whenever you face trials of many kinds." – James 1:2

The instructions that James laid out in chapter one of his book challenges believers in what most would consider a very confusing way. To accept trials in the form of sickness, loss of job, or loss of relationship, as "pure joy" is almost absurd. How can a person consider it a joy when bad things happen to them?

James' words can be literally viewed as very insensitive, but if one reads further they will see that James' thoughts ran much deeper. Verses 3 and 4 read as follows:

"...because you know that testing your faith develops perseverance. Perseverance must finish its work so that you may be mature and complete, not lacking anything." – James 1:3-4

These two verses complete the point that James was attempting to make. Trials in life are often thought or spoken of as "tests." It's more common to hear the words "you're really being tested," than it is to hear "you're really going through a trial." From a Christian standpoint these words are forever intertwined. Trials and tests go hand in hand and should be acknowledged as unique individual opportunities for our faith to grow.

James states that in the midst of trials our faith is tested. A tested faith leads directly to the development perseverance, and through the building of perseverance we are made complete, not lacking anything. In other words, trials that come along in life are essential for our faith to grow and mature.

When people train with weights there is usually some pain involved. Many experience it during the actual training process, and if you're older, like me, you tend to notice it the following day as well. Pain associated with weight training is accompanied by greater strength. The trials faced here on earth are no different. Every trial offers an opportunity to build perseverance which in turn leads to spiritual maturity. As one grows in spiritual maturity the result culminates into a stronger relationship with God.

When hardships or trials come along in life they are always viewed as negative events, but through them amazing things can happen. People are generally shaken by difficult circumstances and many are left wondering which way to turn. It's especially through these moments that God stands waiting for us with His arms open wide. He becomes the sole source of love, comfort, and support we'd ever need.

Whether you're currently facing a trial in your life or not, take a moment to turn to God now. Allow your faith in Him to build the foundation for an eternal relationship in heaven. He's waiting!

Prayer

Father God, I am sorry for all of the times that I've become to busy to recognize all of the wonderful blessings from You. Please forgive me.

Please allow me the strength and wisdom to face my trials in life. Guide me along my journey with You, and help our relationship become one that will be cherished into everlasting life in heaven. Amen.

CHAPTER

2

A Major Setback

Chapter 2
A Major Setback

Our youngest son Todd serves in the U.S. Army. We were fortunate to have him come to visit with us in early June. He'd been in the process of transitioning into a new position and was able to break away for a few days.

At the end of his visit, June 6th to be exact, my wife and I were taking him to Columbus, Ohio, to catch a flight home. We hadn't driven very far when I felt my heart begin to flutter and beat out of rhythm. I'd gone into atrial fibrillation. I was blessed in the fact that this happened directly in front of a hospital in Bucyrus, Ohio, so we immediately stopped at the emergency room.

The physician that treated me ordered a series of blood tests and one in particular showed I was positive for blood clots. I was then sent for a CT scan of my chest area which confirmed the blood test results. There were several blood clots found within my left lung.

At that point, I was immediately started on a blood thinner called Heparin through an IV. Due to the nature and number of clots, it was decided to transport me to a larger hospital located in Mansfield, Ohio, and I was admitted upon my arrival.

I was treated by two different physicians in Mansfield, a cardiologist, and a pulmonologist. One of them mentioned the fact that 90% of blood clots in the lungs actually originate in the legs. That said, he ordered a special test called a Doppler scan to determine if the clots were actually forming in my legs and if there were others. The test came back negative for any clots which left them puzzled over my condition.

The length of my hospital stay was 6 days. My heart eventually returned to its normal rhythm and I was released. The cardiologist prescribed for me a blood thinner called Coumadin. He'd also mentioned that it could likely take several months for the clots to be totally dissolved.

Over the next few weeks I felt pretty well, but when July rolled around things changed. The fever that had plagued me through April and May had returned. I became very fatigued in most physical activities to the point that going up and down stairs wore me out.

-Jim

I was once again at work when my sister Angie called about my father. Part of me was really beginning to wonder if there was a correlation between my place of employment and his ailments! This time my sister informed me that our father was in an emergency room in Bucyrus, Ohio, and his heart was out of rhythm.

I soon found myself making the same trek north with the same anxieties I'd experienced a few months earlier. I began trying to answer the many questions that filled my mind. Why was his heart out of rhythm? Was he having another heart attack? I work in the medical field and carry a little knowledge, but things weren't adding up for me.

Unable to solve the situation on my own, I soon turned to God in prayer. I found those moments with God to be both peaceful and comforting. His presence with me that afternoon was unmistakable. I began to feel a sense of calmness wash over me and my worries began to dissipate. All of this was a reflection of God's grace, love, and faithfulness for me.

When I'd arrived at the emergency room, my brother and two sisters were in the waiting area. They quickly brought me up to date with his condition by telling me there was a distinct possibility that he had blood clots (pulmonary embolisms) in his lungs. Upon hearing those words the seriousness of the situation magnified tenfold. I knew that pulmonary embolisms could be very dangerous and life threatening if not immediately treated.

The physician treating our father suggested a CT scan of the lung area to rule out or solidify the speculation of blood clots. Either way, it was very difficult waiting and anticipating the results. We did our best to keep focused on the positives and discussed the unknown road ahead.

After the lengthy wait, we'd finally received news that confirmed the physician's suspicion. The CT scan revealed several blood clots lodged within our father's left lung. Due to the sheer number and nature of the clots, the physician decided to transfer him to a larger hospital in Mansfield, Ohio. The ironic thing about this was the fact it was the same hospital in which I completed much of my medical training while in college. I was very familiar with the organization and had utmost confidence he'd receive great care.

When it was time to transport my father, an ambulance and crew arrived to move him. My mother was offered and quickly decided to ride along in the ambulance. The rest of us climbed into our own vehicles to make the 40 minute journey to Mansfield.

The day had grown very long and none of us had eaten. Without knowing what the rest of the day had in store, my brother, two sisters, and I decided it would be best to stop for something to eat. It was the first time that any of us could recall when it was just the four of us sitting down together for a meal. We were all married and usually joined by our spouses and children in this type of setting. As unique as it was, I'll always cherish those moments together. It was like going back in time, back to when we were young kids chasing big dreams.

Our mother was seated next to our father when we'd arrived at the hospital. The initial plan was to admit him, but the census was high and no beds were available. After another lengthy wait, he was eventually admitted to the cardiac floor of the hospital where a very pleasant nurse was assigned to him. She instructed all of us in regards to the next steps of treatment. This included being seen by a cardiologist and pulmonologist who'd both be in the next morning.

The rest of our evening together was spent discussing the events of the day and wondering what lied ahead. Despite the seriousness of the situation, my father was able to keep the conversation light and full of his usual humor. We eventually said our goodbyes before leaving the hospital. It had been an incredibly long day for everyone, especially our father.

The night was a mere blink of an eye before we found ourselves loading back into our vehicles with many of the same questions and worries from the day before. Why were blood clots becoming lodged in his lungs? Where were they coming from? Is he going to be alright?

Throughout the day, there were many visitors that stopped by to visit my father. It was great to see all of the love and support he'd received from family and friends. There are simply no words to describe what it meant to be surrounded by loved ones during those days.

Two of the most important visitors that day were physicians. Upon studying the blood tests, CT scan, and other items listed in his medical chart, the physicians collaborated on a plan of treatment. My father would be kept on the blood thinner called Heparin. It was given in the form of an IV that ran continuously. He'd also be scheduled for another test called a Doppler ultrasound. It was a test to be performed on the blood vessels in his legs to determine if there was any evidence of the clots originating there. The physicians discussed how most blood clots in lungs originate in the legs and they needed to see if there were any others.

The physicians speculated the cause of my father's heart being out of rhythm was probably a direct result of the blood clots. One of them explained how clots actually pass through the heart before entering and becoming lodged in the lungs. This alone could cause it to go out of rhythm.

Later that evening, when the Doppler ultrasound had been completed, the physician was making his final rounds and stopped in with the results. There was no evidence of blood clots found forming in his legs. It was good news that nothing was found, however, it left no clear explanation for what was actually causing the clots.

After 6 long days my father was finally released from the hospital. His heart was back to its normal rhythm and he was feeling fairly well. The physician informed him that he'd be given a prescription for a blood thinner called Coumadin. He also stated that the clots in his lungs were stable and he was in no immediate danger, but it could actually take several months before they were totally dissolved.

Moments with God

"Be still and know that I am God." −Psalms 46:10

It was the fall of 1997. My beautiful wife Valerie and I were excited to be expecting our first child together. We'd been married for nearly three years and eagerly awaiting the unknown challenges and blessings that lied ahead of us as parents.

Valerie was scheduled for a routine visit with her doctor to check on the progression of her pregnancy. It was nothing out of the ordinary so I hadn't made any special arrangements to accompany her. When things were finished she immediately called me. Not long into our conversation I noticed a sense of worry in her voice. As our discussion continued Valerie revealed that her physician was concerned about the baby and wanted her to have an ultrasound to check on the status of our little one.

Needless to say, my heart literally sank at this news. I was very concerned for Valerie, but also our baby we'd been so eagerly anticipating. Anxious thoughts and many questions swirled in my mind as I attempted to remain focused at work. Why did this have to happen to our baby? What could possibly be wrong?

While making the journey home that evening, I decided to stop by a local Christian bookstore. I desperately needed to find something, anything, to find comfort for my worries toward this troubling news. I knew the bookstore was an abundant resource of God's word. What better way to find comfort and hope than with our risen Savior?

I entered the store and was greeted by the clerk with a warm smile and welcome. I slowly began to walk up and down the aisles of books, music, artwork, and other trinkets that lined the shelves. I found a plethora of support that surrounded me from all angles, but I struggled to find anything that spoke to my specific needs.

After a short time, I grew disappointed with my futile effort to find something and began walking to the front of the store to leave. As I was about to step out of the door something caught my eye. It was a small refrigerator magnet with a peaceful nature scene. Although it was small in size it stood out like a beacon in the night. I immediately picked it up to read this verse:

Be still and know that I am God." - Psalm 46:10

My eyes welled up with tears while reading the passage. I soon felt an indescribable sense of calmness and peace sweep across me that could only have come from God. The revelation by Him in this passage was very clear and gave me the comfort I was seeking in a very simple yet powerful way.

I purchased the magnet and hung it on our refrigerator as soon as I walked through our front door. It served as a constant reminder during those difficult days that regardless of how hard things became, I needed to remain still and allow God to be God. I couldn't allow myself to worry about our unborn child or anything else for that matter. I simply needed to trust in the fact that Valerie, the baby, and I were all in His care. Regardless of what lay ahead of us, He loved us and would provide the strength and understanding to see us through.

The next week Valerie went for the ultrasound and everything checked out fine with our baby. A few short months later we welcomed into the world our first child, Bryanna Jeanne, a perfectly healthy little girl. The entire journey was both a lesson and blessing I'll cherish forever.

There are many instances throughout our lives that God seeks our stillness. In fact, He seeks our stillness with everything. By remaining still we are fully trusting God's will for our lives. These words are certainly easy enough to acknowledge and say, but can be very difficult to put into action. There are too many instances when we fall short and rely on our own human instincts to fix or make things better. By going into this self-reliant mode instead of turning to God and remaining "still," we are not truly being obedient to His word or commands. We ultimately find ourselves stuck in the rut of our own human nature not being able to escape our troubles.

When I first received word that my father was back in the hospital, my medical background and human nature desperately wanted to fix everything. My drive to the hospital was very long and arduous. It wasn't until I entered into a true state of "stillness" through quiet prayer that I allowed God to intervene. I soon found myself showered by His calming love that extinguished the flames of worry and fear which had engulfed my soul.

Prayer

Heavenly Father, please fill me with Your strength and wisdom. Teach me Your ways. Help me to recognize my own weakness and to remain "still" in You. Guide me in this journey to become less of me and more of You in all of my thoughts, actions, and words. Amen.

CHAPTER

3

Bad News

Chapter 3
Bad News

During the first week of July my strength really began to deteriorate. I simply didn't have enough stamina to do much of anything. I'd also developed another low grade fever. On July 6th I was taken back to the emergency room in Mansfield.

Another CT scan was performed and 28 different vials of blood drawn. The CT scan showed no changes to the existing clots and no new clots had formed. All of my blood tests came back with normal readings.

Upon the results of these tests two different physicians agreed I should be released to go home, but the question remained, why was I getting the fevers, and where were the clots coming from? At my wife's persistence, a CT scan of my abdomen and pelvis was completed before I was sent home. We left with a hope that an answer to everything would soon be revealed.

We were about a half hour into the journey home when our cell phone rang. The call was from a hematologist in Mansfield. He'd received the results of the abdomen and pelvis scan and wanted to meet with us the next day to go over the results. We had no idea what was in store for me.

The next day my wife and I made our way back to Mansfield. When we arrived it wasn't long before the physician came into the room and sat down. He said "I have good news, but also some very bad news. The good news is we found where your clots are coming from, but what's causing them is very unfortunate. You have a massive tumor about the size of a Nerf football in your left kidney. It has grown out of your renal artery and into the vena cava. It has grown upward beyond your liver and just below your diaphragm located about 2 inches from your heart. I'm very sorry, but we can't do anything for you."

I had no idea this tumor was growing inside of me. After the initial shock of the news I proceeded to question if chemotherapy or radiation would help. He responded that this particular type of tumor was resistant to both. He didn't believe that either one would be an effective treatment for me.

I then asked about the possibility of seeing someone at the James Cancer Center in Columbus, Ohio. My wife had been diagnosed and treated for breast cancer there in 2004. It was both a wonderful and successful experience so there was no hesitation in this request. He was very kind and able to schedule an appointment with a kidney specialist the very next week. He then wished us the best as we left his office for the long drive home.

-Jim

There really isn't a way to physically or emotionally prepare for unexpected bad news. It doesn't matter how strong of person, age, race, or sex; unexpected bad news can turn a perfect day into one full of anguish and turmoil.

It had been a wonderful summer day on July 7th, 2008, when I'd received the phone call with the bad news about my father. I was in the middle of enjoying a week of vacation with my wife and children. We'd taken them to a drive-in movie the night before and were enjoying an afternoon of lounging around in our pool. We were having an absolutely great time together.

At the other end of the line was my youngest sister Jennifer, and from the tone of her voice it didn't take very long to realize something was terribly wrong. Jennifer's voice was trembling when she choked out the words, "I've got some bad news Jeff. Dad's CT scan showed an inoperable tumor."

In an instant I broke down sobbing. It felt as if though the entire world was caving in around me. When finally able to gather my thoughts I asked for more details about the tumor. Jennifer discussed how it was very large in size consuming nearly his entire left kidney, and was growing upward in his abdomen toward his heart. The physician stated there was nothing he could do, but was able to set up an appointment for a second opinion at the James Cancer Center in Columbus.

Upon hanging up the phone I proceeded to break the news to my wife. Valerie is an incredible human being. Outside of her natural beauty I've always acknowledged her as an angel sent directly from God. There are countless ways I could describe my love and admiration for her, but the word "angel" describes her best. On that particular day my angel became my rock to lean on, and shoulder to cry on. She truly lived up to being my best friend and I'll never forget it.

The emotions I experienced through the rest of that day ranged from a total sense of helplessness, to moments of somber reflection. My thoughts wandered between questions of what life would be like without my father, to the countless wonderful moments spent with him. My stomach became an unrelenting knot of anguish and pain. I waited desperately for someone to wake me from the terrible nightmare, but it never happened.

That evening our youngest son Brenner was to attend his very first soccer practice. Valerie offered to take him, but I really needed the time to piece things together in my head. As I watched him practice I was flooded with fond memories of playing ball when I was young and seeing my father on the sidelines or in the stands. Why did this have to happen to him? Why now? Why our family?

Later that night I was able to have a phone conversation with my brother Todd. We discussed the news we'd received and the difficult road ahead. As we talked, a certain memory of my father flashed through my mind. It was so vivid that I instantly began sharing the story with my brother as it played out before me.

When I was young my father would spend many evenings tossing the football with me. I loved to throw the ball with him. He knew I had a passion to play and his time spent with me only fueled it even more.

During those moments of throwing with him there were several occasions when the ball slipped through my hands causing a direct hit to my stomach area. Most of the time it wasn't an issue, but if the ball struck me just right the wind would be knocked out of me. In an instant I'd be on the ground squirming in pain while attempting to catch my breath. My father would ensure I was alright before getting a little chuckle over the situation.

I told my brother the key to this story wasn't the fact that my father would get a chuckle every now and then over me getting my wind knocked out. Rather, when we resumed throwing the ball he never slowed things down to make it easier for me. He'd continue throwing with the same velocity and at times a little harder teaching a valuable lesson along the way. The lesson goes something like this:

Jeff, life is going to be difficult at times. Hardships are going to come along and hit you right where it hurts. Don't ever assume or expect that things will automatically lighten up for you because of the hardship. What's important is to always pick yourself up, catch your breath, and continue on your journey.

My brother was stationed in Kansas City at the time. I knew it would be difficult for him to break away from his duties and then it dawned on me how helpless he must have felt. As our discussion drew to a close, I told him I loved him and we'd keep him informed with anything as it became available.

As the day slowly came to a close, my wife and I made the decision to travel to my parent's home the next morning. Arrangements were made for someone to care for our children, as we knew it would be a very difficult and emotional situation to face.

My thoughts wandered in many different directions as I lay in bed quietly waiting to drift off to sleep. Going to sleep was actually the furthest thing from my mind. How are we going to get through this? How much time does he have? The questions seemed to bounce from one side of my head to the other relentlessly reverberating like the bass drum in a symphony. Through the grace of God the questions eventually faded into the darkness of night and I slowly drifted asleep.

Moments with God

Trust in the Lord with all your heart and lean not on your own understanding; in all your ways acknowledge him and he will make your paths straight. – Proverbs 3:5-6

The date was October 23rd, 1992. I was 25 years old and had gone through some very difficult times that year. I will spare you the details, but in essence I had totally hit rock bottom. My search for happiness hit dead ends at every corner, and everything about my life felt awry. Something was missing and regardless of how hard I tried, I couldn't find it.

It was a sunny yet crisp fall afternoon. I was pulling into the driveway of a good friend of my father's. Dave Greenich was the pastor of a Nazarene church in Crestline, Ohio. He knew I'd be stopping by and was busy raking leaves in his yard when I arrived. He met me with a big smile and hug before inviting me into his home.

We sat down and exchanged some pleasantries before discussing the real reason I was there. I'd felt comfortable with Dave so it wasn't long before I opened up to him and shared the turmoil of my life. I was so utterly lost at the time it felt great just to get things off of my chest. I found myself releasing every hurt, trouble, ounce of anger and hopelessness that encompassed my soul.

Dave sat quietly listening to me. When I was finished I noticed tears streaming down his face as if every emotion I felt was flowing through him. I couldn't help but come to the realization that this man really cares about me. He really, really cares.

Dave soon opened his Bible and began to ask me questions. He then handed it to me and asked me to read over a couple of passages. Before long I found myself coming to the realization that God loved me regardless of what I'd gone through, what I'd done, or who I'd become. He loved me right then and there. I was His and it was time for me to put my trust in Him and come home. Upon finishing the different passages, Dave asked me if I wanted to pray. Without any hesitation I replied "Yes!"

We made our way over to the Dave's church which sat next door to his home. I can vividly remember the sun glistening through the church's windows that evening, and how serene everything was. God's presence could be seen and felt.

We slowly made our way to the front of the church where I knelt before the altar and prayed. I can't begin to explain the overwhelming flood of warmth that came across me. The heaviness and burdens that weighed me down were lifted. It was the best I'd felt in as long as I could remember, and it was the single greatest moment of my entire life, no questions asked. My life has become what it is now because of that day and has never been the same.

Over the years Proverbs 3:5-6 has become one of my favorite Bible passages. In the previous chapter I discussed the importance of being "still" and how allowing God to be God has made such an impact on my life. In order to be truly "still" in God's eyes we must fully surrender our trust to Him. We must let go of ourselves completely and allow God to intervene regardless of the situation.

Trusting God and being able to totally surrender ourselves can be two completely different animals. Verse 5 instructs us to *"Trust in the Lord with all your heart."* This doesn't mean to trust Him with a few things of our own choosing such finances or relationships. God wants us to trust in Him with everything and all there is about us. In other words, God wants you to trust with "all your heart."

When my father was diagnosed with this massive tumor in his kidney I found myself asking God questions. Why did this have to happen to him? How are any of us going to get through this? Those questions weren't for me or anyone else to figure out. God's hope for my father and entire family was for us to *"lean not on our own understanding,"* and to trust Him completely regardless the outcome.

Verse 6 tells us to *"acknowledge Him and He will make your paths straight."* If we've fully surrendered our trust in God we must also acknowledge Him in everything we do. He becomes the captain of our ship called life. He is the one that steers us through the calm waters and rough sea. He becomes our guiding light and morning star. To truly fulfill this powerful commitment to God we must forever acknowledge Him with every second of every day. When we are able to trust completely and acknowledge fully, the fog of our lives will be lifted and our paths will be made straight.

Prayer

Dear God, I praise You this day. I give thanks for all of the blessings in my life. I'm sorry I've failed to fully trust You in so many areas of my life. I want to hand You my worries today and to seek Your will in my life. Please open my eyes that I might be more aware of Your spirit working through me. Help me to be a strong voice in my acknowledgement of You and Your ways. I love You Lord. Amen.

CHAPTER 4

The Long Drive Home

Chapter 4
The Long Drive Home

The following day, Friday, July 8th, was one filled with great anxiety for my family. The physician we met with the day before was successful in his attempt to schedule an appointment for a second opinion. I'd be meeting with a kidney specialist the following week at the James Cancer Center located in Columbus, Ohio.

Our oldest son Jeff, and his wife Valerie, made the drive to our home that morning to help us cope with the devastating news. Before long we were joined by our two daughters Angie and Jenny. They spent time doing little chores around the house while being there for support.

Our youngest son Todd, who's a Major in the Army, also made the trip home from Kansas City. It was great to see him again. It's always a special time when we have all of our kids and their families together. It was just unfortunate this visit would be during such difficult circumstances.

I also found myself on the telephone quite a bit that day. Between making appointments and talking to well wishers I'd become a busy man. During some of my quiet moments between visiting with those who were present and talking to others on the phone, I found myself simply staring into space. I just couldn't believe this was truly happening to me.

Later in the day my three oldest granddaughters stopped in for a visit. They'd lost their other grandfather the previous fall to lung cancer and there was grave concern etched across each of their faces. I couldn't help but think about leaving my grandchildren behind. I didn't want any part of it. Not now, it was way too soon.

-Jim

The next morning, my wife and I set off for a somber journey home. I'd made the same trip countless times over the years, but this was most certainly the longest drive home I'd ever experienced. The hour and a half trip turned into what seemed an eternity.

There were very few words spoken between my wife and me during the drive. I was simply doing my best to remain strong amidst all of the hurt, pain, and worry that consumed me. What will I say to him? How could this be happening to him? I found it very difficult to accept that my father could be dying. A part of me was denying it was even taking place.

When we finally arrived, my mother and father greeted us at the door. Normally, our greetings consisted of hugs accompanied with happy smiles and laughs, but things were different that day. The hugs were wonderful and seemed to last much longer, but the smiles and laughs were replaced by quiet sighs and futile attempts to keep from breaking down.

I was taken back by the toll that the stress had taken on both of my parents. They'd visibly aged several years almost overnight. My father was a mere shadow of himself, and my mother appeared to be doing everything possible to hold the weight of the world on her shoulders. Seeing them like this left me speechless. I found myself searching for anything to say that might cut through the heavy sadness.

This was my mother and father whom I loved so very much. Why was this so difficult for me?

My mother soon suggested we should have lunch. "That's it," I thought to myself. "Lunch would certainly help to lighten the heaviness of the discussion we were facing." After some brief small talk on what to eat we decided upon submarine sandwiches. Valerie and my mother volunteered to pick them up leaving my father and me some time to talk alone.

The weather was very pleasant that day so my father and I stepped outside onto the back porch. After some brief moments of awkward silence my father spoke first.

"It doesn't look good, Jeff."

"I know, Dad, I know."

I had trouble making eye contact with him and found myself staring at the ground. It literally took every ounce of energy for me to keep my composure and be strong for him. On the outside I wore a suit of resilience, but I was crumbling to pieces inside.

Our conversation turned toward the office visit from the day before along with the small sliver of hope that remained with the second opinion. It was difficult to grasp that his only hope rested on another person's thoughts and abilities, but this small fraction of hope was the only thing left to hold onto.

After a few other minutes my father's cell phone rang. Being seated right next to him I couldn't help but listen into the conversation. I was able to piece together the fact that it was an old friend of my father's, and there was obvious concern and heartfelt sympathy by this person. My father's voice was very somber as he explained everything. Toward the end of the conversation he said something I'll never forget.

"I've surrendered it all to the hands of the Lord."

A certain part of me was shocked by this statement, yet another part of me wasn't surprised at all. My father is a strong Christian with deep faith and trust in God so it was no surprise that he'd taken such a firm stance. What stood out to me was the fact that he'd been able to lay everything into the Lord's hands so quickly. It was remarkable to witness something so powerful.

The lunch was very good and allowed time for the atmosphere to lighten up a little. Our discussions turned in many different directions allowing us to shift the focus, even if it was only for a short time.

Despite all that was happening the day passed quickly. My father spent time on the telephone talking to different people and received visits by others who stopped by to wish him well. I know this meant a lot to him and was much appreciated by all of us.

One of the phone calls he'd received was from my brother Todd. He'd planned to make the long drive from Kansas City and would be arriving later that evening. Regardless of the dire situation my father was facing, it was great news that Todd would be joining our family soon.

The time spent with my father that day was bittersweet. There was an immense mountain of unknown trials and tribulations ahead for him and our family. The journey would be very long and arduous with very little hope for a happy ending. Regardless of how things went, I knew deep down that he'd be alright. His statement of surrender that I'd witnessed earlier in the day was the only proof I needed. He was in our Lord's care and He alone would see my father through the days ahead.

Moments with God

"He gathers the lambs in his arms and carries them close to his heart." - Isaiah 40:11

Garage sales and flea markets can be wonderful places. I can't say that I've ever been a big fan of them, but on occasion have made stops to browse for new treasures. When I find my vehicle drifting to the side of the road to one of those wonderful sales it's usually my wife that directs me towards the mini outdoor shopping paradise.

On one particular occasion, a church across the street from our home was having a large indoor sale. We didn't have a big agenda that day so my wife and I decided to stop in with our three children to browse for awhile. We spent a better part of an hour sifting through everything from old CD's, books, to kitchen ware. Our children thoroughly loved searching through all of the toys and trinkets on display.

We eventually finished browsing and made our way to the checkout area to pay for the odds and ends we'd gathered. As my thoughts turned to finding the checkout area, I failed to pay attention to how much I was actually carrying. I think garage sales have that kind of effect on a lot of people. One man's junk is another man's treasure!

We'd found the checkout area and were waiting in line when my youngest son Brenner approached me holding one other item.

He looked up at me with an innocent smile and said, "Here Daddy, I want to get this for you. This is me and this is you."

In his hand was a small figurine statue with a wooden base. The figures were of a man bending down to pick a small child up. His hands were around the waist of the child and the child was reaching both arms upward towards the man. On the bottom was the inscription, "Nothing as safe as a father's arms..."

As I held the precious gift in my hands I glimpsed down at Brenner. He had a twinkle in his eyes and smile that was overflowing with love. Within seconds I could feel a lump in my throat and the tears welling up. I gave him a big hug and thanked him for such a wonderful gift. To this day the figurine has its own special place in my office.

Isaiah 40:11 is God's own version of the wonderful gift I'd received. We can find no safer place than in His arms. Just as we take up our own little ones in need of comfort, our Heavenly Father gathers us into His own loving arms during our times of need. He's the eternal comforter in all of life's trials and tribulations. He holds, cradles, and lovingly cares for us with an undeserving infinite abundance.

When I heard my father stating he'd surrendered his cancer to God, I'd truly witnessed him running into the Lord's open arms. He cradled my father and comforted him. He filled him with an incredible sense of peace that became very evident.

This inner peace blessed my father with the ability to view his cancer from a heavenly perspective. It gave him strength and wisdom to see beyond anxieties and fears that are inherent as a human being. My father began see things with a vision of heaven and a future spent in eternity with our Lord, the very One in whose arms he was resting.

Prayer

Heavenly Father, I'm seeking a glimpse of solace in my life today. I need to feel the comfort that can only be found in You. Please guide me through my times of trial and give me the strength to surrender all of my worries to You. May I soon feel the comfort I need right now, the comfort of Your loving arms. Amen.

CHAPTER 5

A Family Portrait

Chapter 5
A Family Portrait

On Sunday morning we attended a church service and many of the people present offered comfort and prayers. After church we returned back to our home where our entire family was gathering to spend the day together.

When our kids were together on Saturday they'd made arrangements for a photographer to stop by on Sunday for a photo shoot of our family. It wasn't often we were all together and with the circumstances I was facing it made perfect sense to do this. Todd's wife Amy couldn't make the trip and we felt bad she wouldn't be in the pictures. As the final touches were made the mood was very somber. I could sense that everyone felt this would be our last shot together.

The appointment with the photographer was scheduled for later in the afternoon so we decided to have a cookout before he arrived. My brother Mark and his wife Chris stopped in to join us. We had a wonderful time without any discussion in regards to my cancer or upcoming appointment in Columbus. We simply took advantage of our time enjoying good food, playing games, and having lighthearted conversations.

The photo shoot came and went much too quickly. Actually, the whole day did. When the kids began leaving for their homes a bit of sadness filled the air along with a quiet that turned our home into a different world. My thoughts at that point were probably the same as the kids, "I wonder how much longer I have." The unknown can turn into a living hell if you allow it...my family didn't and I thank them for that.

-Jim

On Sunday morning I'd received a call from my mother. She relayed the news my brother Todd had made it home safely. She said it was tough at first, but despite the circumstances they'd had a nice visit.

My mother is an amazingly strong woman. She herself had battled breast cancer four years earlier. She had lived the many difficulties my father would go through. Despite being emotionally vulnerable in such a tough situation, I knew she was one tough cookie with an unshakable faith in God. It was a combination built to withstand anything life had to dish out.

Our phone conversation turned toward plans being made for the day. She said a local photographer had been contacted to take some family pictures. When he heard the reason for such a short notice, he graciously agreed to be there.

Throughout the course of that Saturday several phone calls were made to try to coordinate what each person was wearing. Different outfits and colors were planned for each family. The photos would be taken in my parent's backyard. The lawn was well manicured and the landscaping was beautiful. It provided a perfect backdrop and setting for the photos.

My wife, children, and I attended church Sunday morning before making the journey to my parent's home. When we arrived we were greeted with many hugs and hellos from the family. Our children were happy to see their cousins again and quickly made their way to the backyard to play.

The cookout was excellent. My brother and I manned the grill while everyone else helped with setting up tables and preparing the side dishes. My father's brother Mark and his wife Chris stopped in to join us for the cookout. It was nice to visit with them.

The afternoon was full of good times. Although there were many heavy hearts that day, none of us allowed worry or sorrow to rain on our time together. We took advantage of the beautiful weather and spent most of our time outdoors, playing yard games and visiting with each other. God couldn't have provided us with a more perfect day. He blessed us with wonderful food, weather, and many moments made for heaven.

It soon became time to get ready for our family pictures. During that time the mood really seemed to change, everyone became more reserved and quiet. Despite a few minor jokes here and there, the atmosphere was very somber. Like a bolt of lightening, the reality of what our family was facing had come crashing in. With a single blow it had eliminated much of the joy we'd experienced together just hours before.

One by one we followed the photographer's directions as he positioned us for each shot. The overwhelming sadness made it difficult to enjoy what we were doing. Many of us put on smiles worthy enough to produce decent pictures, but behind every smile were thoughts driven by anxiety, worry, and profound sadness.

I found myself wondering if this would be the last time we'd have photographs taken as a family, or possibly be the last chance we'd have to spend a day together. It was very difficult to think about, but was a reality we all had to face. Why did this have to happen? Why him? Why now?

The evening soon faded and it became time to journey back to Columbus. So much of me wanted the afternoon to never end, but I'd found it very difficult to escape the sadness I felt as the day wore on. As hard as it was for me to leave, I needed to get home.

When it was time for our goodbyes, I wanted to hold onto my father forever. For a brief moment I closed my eyes while a memory of a better day flashed through my mind. We slowly pulled from the driveway and my parents stood waving goodbye. As the warmness of tears trickled across my cheeks, with one final wave, we left.

Moments with God

"My grace is sufficient for you; my power is made perfect in weakness." - 2nd Corinthians 12:7

In the second book of Corinthians the apostle Paul suffers from a thorn embedded in his flesh. At some point in our lives we've all experienced the very same type of nagging pain from a similar circumstance. Many of us have experienced a splinter or thorn. The amazing thing about splinters or thorns is that size doesn't matter. Even the smallest can invoke a great amount of anguish and pain.

Although the image of a thorn is what was painted in 2nd Corinthians, it's not certain there was an actual physical thorn Paul was describing. Regardless if there was an actual thorn, some physical or emotional ailment, it extremely bothered Paul and he was seeking God's intervention.

Paul deals with the thorn by asking God on three separate occasions to take his pain away. God's simple response to Paul was that His grace was sufficient for Paul and this thorn situation. One can almost picture Paul standing there with this nagging problem scratching his head while wondering how God's grace was going to fix things. A better part of him was probably upset that God just wouldn't take the thorn and all of the problems it was causing away.

I was experiencing the very same thoughts in my prayerful pleadings to God. I became very much like Paul. I'd believed in God with all of my heart, but couldn't understand why my father was stricken with cancer. Why would God allow this to happen to such a great man?

To find Paul's and my answer we only need to look at the end of Corinthians 12:7. God's power is made perfect in weakness. God chose not to take away Paul's physical pain. Instead, He supplied Paul with an extra dose of grace to cope with his pain. God chose to allow Paul to suffer to further teach Paul more about His power.

Throughout his endurance, Paul came to realize God's true power becomes perfect when we're in our greatest times of need. God isn't always going to take away our suffering whether it's physical or mental, but He will certainly supply us with the grace and strength to make it through.

Prayer

Dear Father, I come to You today seeking Your awesome power. Like Paul, I suffer from thorns in my flesh. Help me to understand Your ways. May Your true power be exhibited through my suffering, whether You choose to one day take my suffering away, or not. I give You thanks for the many blessings in my life. Amen.

CHAPTER 6

One Glimmer of Hope

Chapter 6
One Glimmer of Hope

The following week we made the trip to the James Cancer Hospital in Columbus, Ohio. There was a hope in our hearts they'd be able to do something for me, but we were prepared for whatever the news might be.

When we arrived, I checked in and was shown to the examination room. I was joined by the entourage that made the trip with me. Soon, a young physician came in and introduced himself. He'd previously reviewed my case and told me it was something he wasn't capable of doing. The size of the tumor and involvement with surrounding organs would require an extensive operation. One that went beyond his skills set as a surgeon. He then informed us that one of his partners might be willing to take my case. He was known as an excellent surgeon and if anyone was capable to help me it'd be him. Before leaving the office, I'd received news that my next appointment with his partner had already been scheduled. The physician also set me up for a CT scan of my chest and an MRI of my head to ensure the cancer hadn't spread.

Although the trip to Columbus hadn't provided the results we were praying for, the glimmer of hope was still alive. There still remained a possibility something could be done. Or was there? Why would anyone agree to operate on a tumor that had already been deemed as inoperable by two other physicians?

On the day of my third opinion I was joined by my wife, two daughters, and son Jeff. Todd, my other son, was back in Kansas City eagerly awaiting word from us. After another brief wait we were joined by the physician. I immediately took notice that this fellow looked even younger than his partner. One could about imagine the nervous thoughts going through my head at that point.

When the introductions were completed he jumped immediately into my case. First, he revealed that my CT and MRI results were good and there was no evidence the cancer had spread. This instantly brought a collective sigh of relief from everyone. He then explained the risks involved with an operation of this magnitude, but he would definitely be willing to tackle it. There was another collective sigh with a couple of smiles. Our glimmer of hope had grown a little brighter.

The surgeon then left the room to further review my case with an oncologist that'd also be caring for me. Decisions were being made in regards to chemotherapy treatment. Would this type of tumor respond to chemotherapy? If so, should chemotherapy be done before or after the operation?

It was agreed upon by both physicians that I'd be placed on a new medication called Sutent. Sutent was designed to cut off the blood supply to tumors. The lack of a blood supply results in a stoppage of growth leading to shrinkage of the tumor being treated. Sutent also causes outer layers of tumors to harden into a consistency very much like an orange peel. The hardening of the outer layers helps prevent the cancer from spreading. I was prescribed to be on Sutent for a period of three months. The hope was to shrink the tumor thus making the operation more manageable.

Although the day had laid before me a journey that appeared long and full of uncertainty, I felt like my chances were improving. I was really beginning to sense God intervening and how all of the prayers being lifted were truly making a difference. Not only were prayers being answered, but I'd become more aware of how God would care for me throughout the difficult journey ahead.

-Jim

It was another steamy July afternoon when my wife and children dropped me off at the airport. I was flying to Omaha, Nebraska, to take part in a summer camp for children with parents serving in the military. In 2005, I was fortunate to have had my first children's book published. Its subject matter dealt with children being separated from parents who are called to serve in war. I'd been invited as a guest speaker to share the book and work with the children for a couple of days. Despite everything my family was going through with my father at the time, I was honored to be part of this noble cause.

As I boarded the plane, I couldn't help but think about what would be happening during my time away. My father was due to meet with the second surgeon on the day I'd be flying home. In fact, I'd be in the air somewhere between Omaha and Milwaukee during his scheduled appointment time.

I arrived in Nebraska late that night and was picked up at the airport by the camp director. We visited for awhile before he dropped me off at a hotel in which he'd reserved a room. It had been a long day and I was eager to put thoughts to rest. After a phone call home to my wife to let her know I'd arrived safely, I turned in for the night.

The next morning the camp director picked me up and we made our way to the campground. During our journey I had many questions in regards to the children and how they were coping. The director discussed how important it was to bring these children together in this type of program. All of them had a parent preparing to serve, were currently serving, or had just return from serving in Iraq. In many ways they were alike, but he found that they all dealt with separation in their own unique ways.

That afternoon I spent time with 4 different groups of kids ranging from 7 to 14 years of age. The groups consisted of 15 to 20 kids and each was unique. Some of the children had dealt with deployment of a parent two and three times, and they'd learned to cope with the situation. There were others that hadn't experienced it before and were really struggling with it.

The groups were organized according to age and sex. I met with the younger children before moving onto the older groups. I spent time reading my book "Timmy and the Storm," and then discussed deployment. I'd also given them some pointers on writing and put them through a writing exercise. Everything had gone very well through my first three groups of children. When I worked with the last group which consisted of girls between the ages of 11 and 14, I hit an unexpected snag.

I began by reading my book just as I had with the previous groups. As I made my way toward the end I glanced up and noticed most of them were crying. Having already been an emotional mess with my father's illness, it wasn't long before I felt the warmness of my own tears streaming down my cheeks. Through the grace of God I was able to regain enough composure to finish the book.

After wiping away a few more tears I told the girls, "Its okay to cry. Sometimes things in life can get tough and it's okay to show that emotion. Don't ever be afraid to cry." It was one of the most difficult yet incredible moments. I'll never forget it.

The rest of that day along with the next was spent taking part in different activities with the counselors and children. In my short time with them I'd grown attached to each and every one of them. I wanted so much to take all of their hurt and worry away but knew things were out of my control.

When it was time to leave I found it very difficult for me to say goodbye. It was wonderful to share my book and spend time with those special children. The resiliency and emotional fortitude of some of them was truly amazing. In many of them I saw an image of myself, a simple human being struggling to find peace and cope with a situation totally out of my control. As we drove away from the camp many of their faces and stories flashed through my mind. My only hope was that I'd been able to help them as much as they helped me.

My return trip took me from Omaha to Milwaukee before my final leg to Columbus. As the plane left ground, my thoughts turned back home where my father would be meeting a surgeon for a second opinion. I spent the next hour glancing at my watch every few minutes while hoping and praying there would be good news when the plane landed.

When the plane finally touched down in Milwaukee and taxied to the terminal I immediately dialed my mother's cell phone. She told me the operation was above the surgeon's capabilities, but he had a partner that might be able help. After all of the eager anticipation I was very disappointed we hadn't received the news we'd all hoped for. Thoughts of the unknown road ahead swirled through my mind as I boarded my connecting flight home.

Three days later...

A few days later, I met my parents and two sisters in the surgeon's office for his next appointment. My brother Todd awaited word in Kansas City. None of us knew quite what to expect as we sat quietly waiting. It had been an emotional roller coaster ride and we were prepared as we'd ever be regardless if the news was good, or bad.

When the surgeon came into the examination room we were all taken back by how young he appeared. In fact, he looked young enough to have just finished college. He was very direct when discussing my father's case and carried himself with great confidence. In so many words he stated that he'd seen the previous scans and would indeed perform the operation. He discussed how it'd be quite extensive, but felt with my father's overall health in conjunction with his own experience, a successful surgery was within reach.

The surgeon then stepped out to speak with an oncologist also involved with my father's treatment. Between the two it was decided to put my father on a medication before performing the surgery. He was put on a drug called Sutent in an effort to shrink the tumor and make the surgery less extensive. The oncologist decided the best results would be seen if my father was kept on the Sutent for no less than 3 months. Testing done on other areas of his body showed no sign the cancer had spread so there was no immediate need to rush into surgery.

We left the office that day with a new sense of hope. There was still a very long road ahead for my father, but the mountain that was set before him had become a little bit smaller.

Moments with God

"But those who hope in the Lord will renew their strength, They will soar on wings like eagles; They will run and not grow weary; they will walk and not grow faint." - Isaiah 40:31

It was a hot and humid day in August of 1994. The air was so thick one could almost cut it with a knife. As the sweat continued to pour down my face I kept pushing forward with the hope that I'd make it. I'd been running on this same beaten trail for nearly 6 months training for what I called the race of a lifetime, a marathon. Marathons are considered to be one of the ultimate tests of strength, endurance, and perseverance anyone can go through. It would be 26.2 miles of pavement with a few thousand people and I chasing a common goal, the finish line.

I was very serious in my quest to complete the race. In fact, I was a little crazy. To keep myself motivated I decided to add a unique incentive. I was engaged to my future wife Valerie and our wedding was taking place 20 days after the race I'd been training for. I told Valerie that the wedding would be called off if I didn't finish. As crazy as it sounds it worked out very well. It served as an excellent motivator for me, but more importantly it motivated Valerie to keep me motivated!

As each mile passed that hot August afternoon I did his best to keep focused on the task at hand. I was attempting to complete a 20 mile run, the longest distance I'd ever gone while training. The further I pressed on the more my aches and pains became evident.

After completing 13 miles I noticed a familiar face. It was another runner named John that had been training for the same race. He was also attempting a 20 mile run but had already completed 17. Although we were at different points in our respective runs, we decided to continue toward our individual goals together, stride for stride.

It wasn't long before we began to discuss the different aches and pains we were experiencing. I was puzzled at how well John was cruising along after 17 miles and asked him,

"You've run 17 miles, but you look like you could run forever. How on earth do you do it?"

John responded, "I find my strength from a verse found in the book of Isaiah. It's Isaiah 40:31 to be exact. Whenever I find things getting tough for me during my run I simply recite, "Those who hope in the Lord will run and not grow weary."

John went further to explain the significance of how God strengthens us not only in things as simple as running, but in all aspects of life. It was wonderful to hear John's passion. He was a true warrior for Christ. We finished John's final 3 miles together before wishing each other the best and parting ways.

The heat continued its dominance as I put my best foot forward to complete the remaining 4 miles. Shortly into the next mile cramps began to invade my lower legs. Unfortunately, I hadn't been able to drink enough liquid to counteract all of the fluid and electrolytes I'd been losing. I was dehydrating at a rapid pace and my muscles were paying the price.

I finally slowed down to a bit of a hobble as the pain became almost too much to bear. Then I remembered what John had mentioned just minutes earlier and began reciting, "Those who hope in the Lord will run and not grow weary." Before long I found myself in the middle of a prayerful conversation with God. My hobble soon turned into a jog and shortly thereafter I was once again moving at my regular pace.

Miles 18 and 19 passed by quickly, and when mile 20 came around I began thanking and praising God. My strength had been renewed and I'd accomplished my goal. It was an unforgettable moment that will continue to serve as a constant reminder of God's love for me.

One of the greatest things we can accomplish on earth is learning to put our hope in God. It's an inevitable fact that each one of us will face mountains in life that are too difficult to climb. We need only to turn to Him. He will provide us with the courage to go on. He will be the one that "renews our strength." We might be facing a loss of a job, have relationship issues, or even a terminal illness. Regardless of the circumstances, the strength and renewal we'll receive from God will see us through anything. All that He wants is our hope.

When my father was diagnosed with cancer he immediately turned his cares, worries, and sickness over to the Lord. Surrendering this hardship was not only a testimony of his trust in God, but also his hope. It was through his hope that God gave him the strength and peace to carry on when he was informed the tumor was inoperable. Without hope in God I don't how he or any of us would have made it. Time and time again, our hope was kept alive and God continued to "renew our strength."

Where are you today? Are you standing before a mountain of problems and aren't quite sure which way to turn? It's time to put you hope in God. Allow him to "renew your strength" to carry on. There's nothing to lose and only an eternity of peace to gain.

I continued training for the marathon and I finished the race on "wings like eagles." Upon crossing the finish line, I found my future bride and kissed her. I then placed the medal I'd received around her neck and asked her if she'd marry me. As the tears streamed down her face she smiled and said, "Yes." My beautiful wife Valerie and I were joined in marriage on December 3, 1994.

Prayer

Dear God, I often find myself growing weary of the daily grind. Far too often I rely on my own strength to make it through. I want to see You in a new way Lord. I pray that through Your guidance I'll be free to put all of my hope in You. For it is through You my strength is renewed. I need You my Lord, please renew my strength today. Amen.

CHAPTER 7

Enduring the Wait

Chapter 7
Enduring the Wait

On August 4th, I made a return trip to Columbus for a biopsy on the tumor. The physicians needed to determine the type of kidney cancer I had before actually starting me on the Sutent which was discussed during my last appointment. The biopsy revealed the tumor was exactly what they'd expected, Clear Cell Renal Carcinoma.

I was told that this type of cancer does not respond to regular chemotherapy or radiation therapy. The only hope to control it was the drug Sutent. The original plan was to keep me on it for three months to help make the operation more manageable. If the tumor reacted the way they'd predicted, then there would be some consideration to keep me on it for an additional three months.

My first couple of months on Sutent went very well. In early September my wife and I traveled to Kansas City to visit Todd and his wife Amy. I had very little side effects on the trip other than being fatigued from time to time. I did so well that we thought it would be nice to schedule a trip to the ocean.

My wife and I love the ocean. We enjoy it so much that we try to get there a couple times a year. Our anniversary was September 24th and we thought it would be a great reason to go. Not long after we'd discussed planning a trip, my brother-in-law called to see if we'd join them for a week in Hilton Head, South Carolina in early October. Before fully committing, I contacted my physician to be sure it would be okay for me to go. The physician was pleased with my progress on the Sutent and gave me the green light to go.

On October 6th, we were heading south. Our trip to Hilton Head was very nice. We had a great time visiting, shopping, and taking walks on the beach. My energy was low and I didn't seem to last long on those walks, but they were very enjoyable. The combination of the Sutent and sun were the two culprits that seemed to drain my energy. Fortunately, I was able to sneak a nap here and there to keep up with everyone.

On one particular day, we awoke to rain. We didn't want it to dampen our spirits so we loaded the car and made our way over to Savannah. It was a great idea because Savannah was wonderful. We thoroughly enjoyed the beauty and history of the city, and spent most of the day sight seeing and shopping. It was a memorable time for all of us.

By the end of the week I was ready to leave. The condo we stayed in was on the third floor with no elevator in sight. Having to climb three stories of stairs for a week was difficult and really wiped me out.

It was surely a bittersweet moment when we loaded up to go. I'd tried to keep my mind off the cancer that week, but every once in awhile a thought would sneak in. Is this the last time Barb and I will see the ocean together? Was this our last anniversary? I did my best to fight through the negative thoughts, but once in awhile I needed a reassuring hug. I thank God for my wife and family who were always there to give me those hugs.

-Jim

The long wait posed by my father's physicians was very understandable, but at the same time difficult to accept. I understood the medication (Sutent) would serve as an integral piece of his treatment, but I didn't expect he'd be kept on it for up to 6 months. Why would they take a chance like this on a tumor the size of a small football located in such a vital area of the body?

As difficult as it was to accept the plan of attack, it was even tougher to watch how the cancer and Sutent affected my father. By living an hour and a half away I didn't have the opportunity to see my father very often. I did my best to talk with him each day, but my phone conversations didn't always paint the overall picture of his health. It was a trip back home in early August that became the eye opener for me.

Our family traveled back to New Washington for our niece's birthday party. It was made extra special as my sister and her husband reserved the town swimming pool for a couple of hours. The weather was beautiful and everyone was excited about the unique opportunity of a pool party.

When I first saw my father that afternoon I was astonished by the amount of weight he'd lost since I'd last seen him. The weakness I felt in our embrace only confirmed what my eyes were telling me. A lump slowly formed in my throat as I held him. The reality of my father in the middle of the fight for his life had finally set in.

My father seemed exhausted and very reserved that evening. He took part in all of the festivities, but was more or less confined to a chair the entire time. Every now and then I'd see a smile from him, but it was painfully obvious he was physically weak and his mind was in another place.

Later that night, when we'd returned to our home, I was really struggling with my father's condition. I remember weeping and telling my wife that he didn't resemble himself anymore. Throughout my younger years I'd always thought of him as strong and invincible, and I carried those same thoughts into adulthood. The cancer had stolen the strength and vigor I'd grown accustomed to, and turned him into a mere shadow of himself. It was an extremely difficult thing to see.

When September came around the time seemed to move in slow motion. Much of it was probably due to anticipation of my father's progress from taking the Sutent. My parents decided to vacation in South Carolina to celebrate their anniversary. It was good for them to get away, even for only a week. They both loved the ocean and it was a perfect chance for them to place their worries aside for awhile.

Saturday, October 3, 2008...

I'm an avid fan of Notre Dame Football. The university located in South Bend, Indiana, is a 4 hour drive from our home. Over the past several years I've attempted to attend at least one game each season. I'd been fortunate to have found some good connections to tickets which can be difficult to find at times. My father had traveled with me to several of those games and we'd shared some great memories.

In August of that year, I learned I'd be getting tickets for a game the first part of October. Not knowing if it would be the last opportunity to take my father to a game, I called to tell him the good news. He told me he definitely wanted to go, but it would depend on how he was feeling at the time. I fully understood the circumstances and realized it probably wasn't going to work out.

When the day came to make plans for the trip I made another call to my father. My parents had just returned from their trip to South Carolina and he was still attempting to regain strength. Realizing that walking short distances was tough, and climbing stadium stairs would be very difficult, he decided not to go. The decision was with great reservation, but we knew it would be best for him to stay home.

I then approached a good friend of mine, Scott Campbell. I attend church Scott, and over the past few years have taught a Sunday school class with him. I have utmost respect and appreciate him as a friend and brother in Christ. When he agreed to go I knew it would be an enjoyable day.

The weather in South Bend that day was simply spectacular. The leaves were beginning to change color and the Notre Dame campus had become a little slice of heaven here on earth. After taking in some of the historical sites on campus, Scott and I made our way into the stadium. Our seats were situated in the northwest side of the stadium. They were in perfect position to see one of my father's favorite parts of going to games, watching Notre Dame's marching band make their way to the stadium.

The band traditionally starts near the steps of the administration building and marches across campus. The sound of the fight song and chants send chills up the spine as they echo through the various dorms and school buildings. Large crowds form to cheer on the band's arrival, while others march alongside and behind the band itself. It's truly an amazing spectacle to see.

Scott and I positioned ourselves at the top of the stadium. As I heard the drums and horns in the distance I grabbed my cell phone and dialed my parent's phone number. I'd talked with my father a couple of times earlier in the day so I knew he'd be there. When he picked up the phone I explained that we were at the top of the stadium waiting for the band. I told him that I could hear them in the distance and they'd be arriving soon. His voice met me with a mix of excitement and the sentiment of wishing he was there. When the band neared the stadium it became difficult to hear him on the end of the line. I told him to just close his eyes and listen while picturing himself there with me. With tears streaming down my face I held the phone out toward the wonderful sounds of the Notre Dame Victory March. For a brief moment he was there, and together we'd forged memory I'll cherish forever.

Scott and I enjoyed the game and shared many laughs together that day. It was a special trip for both of us. As we pulled out of the parking lot for the 4 hour journey home I remembered my father's last words before saying goodbye on the phone, "Maybe next year...maybe next year."

Moments with God

"He will not let your foot slip-he who watches over you will not slumber." - Psalm 121:3

The latter half of the past century provided a technological boom that would leave the great inventors Franklin, Edison, and Bell scratching their heads. One of those inventions was the computer. The computer world then brought us email which has become one of our greatest forms of communication.

Recently, I stumbled across one of those insightful email messages that I found quite interesting. It contained a powerful message that was very straight forward and meaningful. It was an old Cherokee legend about a young warriors "Rite of Passage."

During this major event of the young Indian boy's life he is walked deep into a forest by his father. Once they've cleared themselves of any other sign of man, the father places a blindfold over the boy's eyes and leaves him alone. The task becomes much more difficult as the boy is required to sit alone until he sees sunlight glimmering through his blindfold the following morning. He is also instructed to not utter a single word. If he survives the night he completes the "Right of Passage" and is recognized by the tribe as a man.

The young boy was no different than most people would be in the same circumstances, they were usually terrified. All through the night different sounds of wild animals would be heard creeping nearby. At times he wondered if it was another human being who wished to cause him harm. It didn't matter how many different sounds or worrisome thoughts he experienced, he was required to remain upright and still without removing the blindfold. Only then could he become a man.

When the darkness of night finally surrendered to the beams of sunlight at dawn the boy could remove the blindfold. It was at that precise moment that he discovers his father who'd been sitting on the stump next to him. He'd been watching over his son the entire night, protecting him from any possible harm.

This wonderful story can be compared directly God's relationship with His people. Our lives will be blessed with many good days, but there will also be trials and tribulations. It's important to remember that our heavenly Father watches over us at all times, good or bad. He'll rejoice in our bright days of happiness, and provide comfort and peace during dark days of trouble. God's unconditional unwavering love will guide us through our "Right of Passage" on earth as Christians until we reach our eternal home with Him in heaven.

Prayer

Heavenly Father, I come to You today with worship and adoration. I praise You for Your unending grace, love, and faithfulness to me. Thank You for keeping watch over me through my Christian journey here on earth. Please continue to provide opportunities for me to grow and mature into the Christian You long for me to become. I love You Father. Amen.

CHAPTER

8

Preparing for Surgery

Chapter 8
Preparing for Surgery

The latter part of October brought with it another birthday for me. On October 19th, we celebrated my birthday with a carry-in chicken BBQ at Jeff & Valerie's home in Columbus. It couldn't have been a nicer day.

One of my favorite joys of life is when our family gets together. Whether it's a birthday, anniversary, holiday, or quick visit, they're all great. It was special to be celebrating my birthday that day, but I had trouble escaping the questions looming in the back of my mind. Would this be our last celebration together? Would this be my last birthday?

We had a really terrific time and were sorry it couldn't have lasted longer. My feelings of being mortal were really beginning to sink in. I found myself sitting and reflecting on the things to come. We made plans for one more family get together for Halloween on the last weekend in October. It was nice to have another date in the near future to look forward to.

On October 21st, I was back in Columbus for a CT scan to see if the Sutent had any effect on the tumor. It wasn't long after we'd arrived back home when I'd received a call from the surgeon who said, "The tumor has grown. It's now about an inch from your heart and we need to get it out of there soon. I am in the process of putting together a team of surgeons and will call you back when everything is set up."

The next day, while trying to cope with the news that the tumor had grown, I received another call from the surgeon. He told me he was able to assemble a team and I was to report to the hospital on November 5th. The team of physicians would include the lead surgeon, a heart surgeon, a liver specialist, and a host of other resident physicians and medical personnel. It was without a doubt that God had His hand in the organization of this team in such a short period of time.

The surgeon went on to explain there would be 2 days of prep before the operation. The surgery itself would be at least a six hours long due to the involvement of the tumor with the kidney and other vital organs. Because the tumor had grown so close to the heart the procedure would involve cracking my chest to bypass my heart, very much like an open heart procedure. He reiterated the fact it was a very serious and delicate operation with many unknowns.

When the conversation was over I thought, "WOW!! So this is it." Part of me was glad to finally be in the position to have the tumor removed, but there was also a fear of the surgery. If I made it through the surgery, what were the chances the cancer hadn't spread to other areas of my body? If there's a tumor the size of a Nerf football in my kidney that's growing inside one of the main vessels and is an inch from my heart, how long do I have? What are my odds of surviving the operation?

Fear was really beginning to set in. My entire family was doing their very best to remain positive, not letting me even begin to say anything negative. I pray that God will continue to bless them for their great fortitude. I don't know what I'd have done without their encouragement.

Outside of the support and encouragement from my family I did a lot of praying during the days leading up to my surgery. There were also prayers being lifted up across the United States and abroad for me. My son Jeff mentioned a prayer chain he'd been involved with that had people praying from New York, Texas, and Oregon.

There was also a pastor spending a year at Jeff's church from Campinas, Brazil. Pastor Ernesto Ferreira was part of the largest Nazarene church in the world with over 8,000 members. During one of his visits he assured our family that prayers were also being lifted from his church in Brazil. It was a very humbling experience to know how many people were praying for me.

-Jim

On the morning of my father's birthday my good friend Scott and I took part in a half-marathon. The weather was a little cool at the start, but gradually warmed to be quite comfortable. We had an enjoyable time during the run which I'd personally dedicated to my father.

Like most long races I'd taken part in, there came a point when I began to notice little aches and pains. As those moments arose, I simply spent a couple of moments to reflect on what my father had endured and found the inspiration to keep going. I wasn't able to finish with the time I'd hoped for that day, but finished stronger than I'd expected.

The afternoon brought another chance for my family to get together. The celebration of my father's birthday was full of mixed emotions. For most of us it was difficult not to wonder if it would be his last birthday celebration. As the events and our time together passed by I found it more difficult to remain upbeat.

One of the toughest things for me was watching our children as they interacted with my father. They understood he had cancer and was very sick, but some of them were too young to really grasp the magnitude of the situation. When the festivities of the day came to an end a better part of me was happy. There was another part that wanted the day to last forever.

A couple of days later my father went back to the hospital for a CT scan. We'd been hoping and praying throughout his time on Sutent the tumor would respond and shrink in size. When we received the news it hadn't and actually grew in size, our family was struck with a feeling of utter helplessness. The three month wait we'd endured seemed totally fruitless. Many of us pondered the possibility of cancer cells escaping the confines of the tumor to other parts of his body. The speed at which a surgical team was assembled only amplified the seriousness of the situation.

A week before my father's scheduled surgery I went for my yearly physical. It was nothing out of the ordinary and something I'd done over the past several years. There were blood tests run, an EKG, along with every other wonderful thing we get to experience during physicals.

As the physician was wrapping things up he guided me through my blood test results. He said that everything checked out fine, but there was one that was a little off. He then informed me he'd be sending me to a hematologist to be sure there wasn't any underlying cancer.

I nearly collapsed to the floor with the news. All of the emotional stress and anxiety I'd experienced with my father's illness had instantly ballooned. Images of his arduous journey with cancer flashed through my mind as I remembered how it began with a trip to a hematologist.

I can't have cancer! How could this be? I found myself going through the exact same questions all over again. Everything seemed surreal. Could this possibly be happening to me? Do I have cancer too?

My appointment was early in the morning so I returned to work when it was finished. As I struggled to cope with things, I called my wife to break the news. Valerie's concern on the telephone was unmistakable. As we continued to discuss the situation I could tell she was trying her best to remain calm and composed. I found it very hard to hang up the phone at the end of our conversation. Valerie had become my "rock" in life. Not only was she my wife, but also my very best friend. She'd been such a help for me coping with my father's illness, but now I needed her more than ever.

Throughout the rest of the day I felt my focus slip further and further away. I began going through moments of sheer panic and anxiety. My heart would race and breathing speed up until I'd actually begin to bead up with sweat. All I could think about was my family. My children needed me, how would they manage without me?

At 2:30 I'd decided to place a call to my good friend and pastor, Sam Barber. I asked him if he'd have some time for me to stop by his office. Without any hesitation, he agreed to meet with me.

It wasn't long after I'd arrived that Sam could see I was shaken. I sat down and immediately began to explain the recent news of my blood tests. The tears started to pour out of my eyes as I sobbed in utter helplessness. I discussed how hard it had been to shoulder my father's illness and remain positive and strong. The news I'd received on my lab tests was my tipping point, I simply couldn't bear to carry any more.

Sam walked over to my chair and stood behind me. Placing both hands on my shoulders he began to pray for me. I'll never be able to repeat his exact prayer, but I'll always remember three important elements. He prayed God's peace, God's mercy, and God's strength for me.

I left Sam's office with a renewed spirit to carry on. The road ahead was as unsure as the moment I'd received the news from my physician, but my time spent with Sam in prayer was a reminder of how much God loved me. Regardless of what the future held, I was His child and He would always be with me.

Moments with God

"I know that my Redeemer lives, and that in the end he will stand upon the earth." – Job 19:25

I've heard it said that the true test of man's greatness is what he grabs for "on the way down." Every living breathing human being will at some point experience a tumultuous event in their life. There's absolutely no way to escape it, difficult events are inevitable for everyone. What defines a person's true character is what they reach for "on the way down" during those dark days.

The Bible gives an excellent example of what to grasp for "on the way down" in the book of Job. Job was a man that had been very blessed. He had seven sons and three daughters, along with a very large quantity of livestock and servants. Outside of the life he'd been so richly blessed, Job was a good man whom walked the straight and narrow. He worshiped and honored God in everything he did. All of these elements put together gave Job the reputation of being the greatest man in the East.

Over the course of a very short period of time this honorable man of God found himself being thoroughly tested. These tests were a direct result of a conversation between Satan and God. Satan had realized God blessed Job with many things in life, but was sure if He'd ever allow anything tragic to happen Job would find fault with God. After some careful thought, God agreed to allow Satan to wreak havoc on anything within Job's life, but he couldn't lay a hand on Job himself.

In a single day Satan managed to destroy everything of value to Job. His children and servants were killed. All of his livestock was also either killed or stolen. In a furious unfathomable chain of events Job lost it all.

Upon hearing the string of horrible news reported to him from firsthand witnesses, Job did something that is both awe inspiring and almost unimaginable. He immediately tore his robe and shaved his head before falling to the ground in worship of God stating:

"Naked I came from my mother's womb, and naked I will depart. The Lord gave and the Lord has taken away; may the name of the Lord be praised."

Job's actions during such torment truly spoke clearly of the trust and faith he had in God. Job most certainly realized how richly his life had been blessed by God, but more importantly was his acknowledgement that God was in complete control of these blessings. It was a truly remarkable and historic statement of faith.

Unfortunately for Job, the story didn't end here. Satan came back to God on a separate day with another agenda. He was still seeking a way to prove a good man such as Job would dare to curse God. Satan discussed how the results of Job's first tests were only a fluke, and that any man including Job would sacrifice every possession to protect his own life. Satan, not willing to give up, was seeking God's permission to personally attack Job himself. God knew Job's heart and gave Satan permission to do so.

Satan obliged and attacked Job with a vengeance. Job's body became covered with open sores from the soles of his feet to the top of his head. The pain was so intense that at one point Job took a piece of pottery and scraped himself with it. Could this have been an attempt to change the focus of the pain from the sores to the self-inflicted scrape?

Job's wife was a witness to all that had happened and her faith in God was clearly slipping. She pleaded with Job, *"Are you still holding on to our integrity? Curse God and die!"*

Job replied, *"You are talking like a foolish woman. Shall we accept good from God, and not trouble?"*

Many of us can read about Job and point to events in which we felt very much like him. Instead of seeing that light at the end of the tunnel we find the tunnel only getting longer. In our human nature we find ourselves asking God, "What are you doing this for? What did I do to deserve this?"

God often operates beyond our realm of understanding with both hardships and blessings. We often overlook the blessings He bestows upon our lives, yet we're quick to place blame or question Him when things go wrong.

My father's cancer battle along with news regarding my own health thrust me directly into Job's shoes. Unfortunately, when it came time to be like Job and praise God for the hardships, I failed miserably. I spent too much time questioning God for my problems. The more I questioned the more blind I became to the many blessings He'd given me. The more I questioned the harder it became to surrender my anxiety and worry over to Him.

My visit with Pastor Sam was a direct result of reaching the end of my rope. Things became too difficult for me to shoulder on my own. Going to Sam's office was a form of surrender for me. Very much like my father's surrender a few months earlier, I found myself doing the same. It didn't mean I wouldn't face anxious moments in the days that lay ahead, but my God was with me. I praise God for giving me the strength to reach out to Him "on the way down."

In the latter part of Job's life he became more blessed by God than ever before. He went on to have seven more sons and three more daughters, The number of livestock he owned grew to numbers not seen before, and he lived to a very old age. So old, that he was able to see his children's children down to the forth generation. It is recorded that Job never cursed God and died a very blessed man.

Prayer

Dear God, I pray that I might have the heart of Job. I know there are going to be difficult days in my life. In those days please guide me to have the spirit of Job, to a day where my questions will become praise. Praise to You my God and the many blessings and hardships that You've allowed in my life. Again, I give You thanks and praise this day, and all days. Amen.

CHAPTER

9

Comfort in God's Word

Chapter 9
Comfort in God's Word

I entered the hospital as instructed on November 5th. The first item on the surgery prep checklist was a blood transfusion. The transfusion was in preparation for the procedures that lied ahead. I was scheduled to go through a kidney clamp procedure on the 6th, and the major surgery was scheduled for the 7th.

The blood transfusion went very well, but I was becoming more apprehensive and worried about the next couple of days. I was concerned about the outcome. What did God have in store for me? How long did I have? Will this be my last Christmas?

I was allowed a few visitors at a time that day which really helped the time pass by. During the quiet time before and after visits I felt compelled to read my Bible. A better part of me wondered if this would be my last opportunity to spend time in God's word. My thoughts were racing and I really didn't know where to start, there are so many great books and verses to choose from. I decided to play "Bible Roulette" and randomly open the Bible. I opened to Isaiah 40.

I began reading the chapter, but really had a hard time keeping focused. I stopped a few different times to clear my thoughts before I was eventually able to finish. Shortly after finishing, my son Jeff came into the room. We made some small talk before he mentioned, "I see you've been reading your Bible. By the way, I have a verse that I want you to read. It's Isaiah 41:10." My Bible had been left open on Chapter 40. I turned one page and asked, "Do you mean this one?"

Needless to say, we were both astonished at what had just transpired.

Jeff immediately said, "Read it Dad!" I took and held the Bible in my hands and the words jumped directly out at me.

"SO DO NOT FEAR, FOR I AM WITH YOU; DO NOT BE DISMAYED, FOR I AM YOUR GOD. I WILL STRENGTHEN YOU AND HELP YOU; I WILL UPHOLD YOU WITH MY RIGHTEOUS RIGHT HAND." –ISAIAH 41:10

Together we marveled at how this all came to be. There are 66 different books in the Bible and roughly 1500 pages. The more we talked the more we'd realized the event was beyond coincidence. God wanted to make a point and He wanted to make it clear. After that wonderful moment I was really beginning to feel good about things.

-Jim

It was just an ordinary day for most everyone I passed during my drive to the hospital. Most people were on their way home after a long day of work to be with their families. I'd found it hard not to envy those people. Here I was, wondering how much time my father had left here on earth. If this would be the last time I had to just sit and talk with him.

I parked my car and made my way into the hospital. I remember passing people ranging from physicians, nurses, and other medical personnel, to visitors who were undoubtedly dealing with their own troubled times. I stepped into my father's room and found him resting in his bed with my mother sitting in a chair next to him. They both seemed to be in very good spirits despite the dire circumstances. I took a seat on the opposite side of the bed next to my father. After a few moments of small talk, my parents discussed what the physician's plans were for the next couple of days and the procedures that lied ahead.

A short time into our discussion, I noticed my father had been reading his Bible. It was opened and laying next to him. He acknowledged that he'd indeed been reading from it and mentioned his "Bible Roulette" methodology. We both chuckled over this unique but effective way of reading God's word. As the discussion faded I pulled a piece of paper from my pocket which contained a Bible verse I'd written down. I'd run across the verse in an email message sent to me earlier in the day. I found great comfort from it and decided to share the verse, Isaiah 41:10, with my father.

I asked my father if I could use his Bible to find the verse, which he quickly obliged with a yes. When he handed the Bible over to me he explained that he'd just finished reading Isaiah 40, and was ready to begin Isaiah 41 when I walked in. He said, "Do you mean this one?" I looked at the pages that were now resting in my hands. He wasn't kidding; Isaiah 41 was right in front of me! Our jaws dropped in amazement at what had happened. We realized it was beyond coincidence. We immediately understood that God had guided us to this powerful book and verse. I handed the Bible back to my father and he read aloud Isaiah 41:10.

"So do not fear, for I am with you; do not be dismayed, for I am your God. I will strengthen you and help you; I will uphold you with my righteous right hand."

Together we'd witnessed what God was surely conveying to us. The words came to life as though He was saying the words directly to us. Isaiah 41:10 filled us with a comfort that afternoon which could only have been experienced through God and His word. It was truly awesome to experience God's comfort in such a wonderful way.

When my father was admitted he was placed in a room with another gentleman. The curtain was always drawn between them, so I never really caught a glimpse of him. There were, however, different moments in which I heard him having conversations over his telephone. I couldn't help but wonder what this gentleman was in the hospital for. Was he also suffering from cancer? Was he scheduled for an upcoming surgery?

Outside of God's revelation to us in Isaiah, the second most memorable moment from the evening was witnessing my father interact with this gentleman. First, you really have to know my father. If you looked up the word friendly in the dictionary his picture would be right next to it. He could strike up a conversation with anyone, anytime, and anywhere. The only other person that comes close to him is my father-in-law. I often wonder if they'd actually been separated at birth.

The interaction began when my father left his bed to use the restroom. Upon his return, he'd made eye contact with the man through a gap between their curtains. The gap in the curtain was all he needed to give a quick "hello" and to introduce himself. I can't remember much of the small talk from the conversation, but at some point my father did something I'll never forget. As they discussed their ailments I heard him ask the man if he knew the Lord. He then took it a step further to let him know that he'd be praying for him.

Here he was, facing a surgery in a couple of days that could very easily take his own life, telling a complete stranger he'd be praying for him. Who knew a simple trip to the restroom would lead to an opportunity to share his faith? He didn't have to say anything to this person, but he spared a few precious moments which very well could have changed this man's life forever. It was a true testament of my father's faith and another moment I'll always remember.

Moments with God

"I am the light of the world. Whoever follows me will never walk in darkness, but will have the light of life." – **John 8:12**

In December of 2004, our family embarked on a trip to Disney World in Orlando, Florida. We traveled with my wife's family to this magical place and had a fabulous time. Disney is wonderful regardless the time of year, but being there during the holiday season was a real life fairytale. With six children all under the age of seven we were kept very busy and shared many wonderful memories.

At the end of the trip we were set to depart Orlando on December 23rd. As we packed the suitcases I'd decided to flip on the news to see if there might possible be any flight delays. Going from Ohio to Florida wasn't an issue, but the directions were now reversed. Ohio can at times get its fair share of bad weather.

A couple of minutes into the newscast, I heard the words "Ohio" and "ice storm" being used in the same sentence. My attention then became totally glued to the television. A major ice storm in central Ohio was the lead story for the national news broadcast. Was this really happening or some kind of joke?

The news spread quickly to the rest of the family and we immediately began making calls to the airport. Amazingly, the initial news we received was good. Most of the flights were on time with very few delays. We finished packing while several questions continued to swirl. Would our flight still be on time when we get to the airport? What kind of weather would be going home to? How long could we be stuck in Orlando?

When we arrived at the airport we immediately checked the flight schedules for any delays. We soon found there'd been a 2 hour delay posted on our flight. The weather was bad and apparently becoming much worse in Ohio.

With six little ones exhausted from nearly a week of fun at Disney our 2 hours were spent attempting to curtail the onset of boredom. We took walks, colored pictures, and rested during the long 2 hours. When the wonderful "fun with kids at an airport marathon" was finally over, we loaded the plane for the 2 ½ hour "fun with kids on an airplane marathon."

The final approach into the Columbus airport produced a somewhat eerie sight. It was sometime after 7 p.m. and the normally well lit city was in complete darkness. It would have been great for an episode of the Twilight Zone. Aside from the occasional flickering lights from vehicles on roads below, Columbus appeared to be completely deserted.

The darkness had been a result of power outages caused by the build-up of ice on power lines. The weight of the ice had also taken a toll on many of the trees, causing large limbs to break and fall across the lines. The strange world of darkness left a feeling of sheer despair and hopelessness. How long would the power be out? How long would the darkness last?

We live in a very blessed nation. This country offers a freedom to chase dreams and achieve things not seen in many other parts of the world. There are distinct opportunities for fame, fortune, and wealth regardless of who you are or where you live. There are very few boundaries for anyone.

Despite how great all of this sounds, the final product is a nation stuck in a rut of materialism. Our lives have become a direct reflection of our success. Many people drive nice cars, live in big houses, and wear name brand clothing. The focus has turned toward keeping up with the neighbors, or in many cases one step ahead. Getting caught up in this kind of lifestyle can lead to a very slippery slope for Christians.

Rather than conforming to what most of the world calls normal, Christians must maintain a focus on God. We cannot allow the wonderful things of life to become like the ice found on the power lines and tree limbs on that cold December night in 2004. Instead we must allow God, "THE light of the world," to be entrenched in every aspect of our daily lives.

The same can be said for the many trials we face in life. Difficult times can also build up like ice on power lines of our spiritual life. Sickness, poverty, loss of job or relationship, can all be culprits if allowed. Just as success and material things can lead us on slippery slopes, so can hard times.

My father's battle with cancer is a great example of remaining focused on God despite the difficult circumstances. He could have easily turned his back and walked away from God, but he didn't. He chose only to grow closer through the reading of his Bible and prayer. These actions not only produced hope and peace for him when things became tough, but it allowed God to use him to share this peace. By running directly to God he found Him waiting with His arms open wide.

Prayer

Heavenly Father, I come to You today in search of Your comfort. I pray for strength and wisdom to run to You in difficult times, rather than run from You. I praise You for the life You've blessed me with, and I give thanks for the comfort I've found in Your word. I love You and honor You my Lord, today and every day. Amen.

CHAPTER

10

God's
Awesome
Revelation

Chapter 10
God's Awesome Revelation

The next morning I was scheduled for the kidney clamp procedure. The procedure involved cutting off the blood supply to the kidney containing the tumor by clamping the vessels leading into it. By cutting off the blood supply to the kidney the tumor's blood supply was also being cut off.

The physicians explained the clamp would cause similar symptoms as a heart attack, but would be taking place in my kidney. My kidney would actually be dying from the lack of blood without an attempt to save it. It was to be very painful, but they ensured that I'd be under heavy sedation.

Before leaving for the procedure, Jeff had shown up with a piece of paper containing the verse Isaiah 41:10. It was printed in very large letters and he pinned it on a bulletin board sitting next to my bed. We huddled together and prayed before the attending nurses and aides wheeled me out of the room for what lied ahead.

While my family waited, another pastor from Jeff's church stopped in to visit with them. Pastor Tim Swanson spent time listening to and discussing with them the different things due to take place over the next couple of days. Before leaving he gathered my family for a time of prayer. He said, "Before I start I want to share a verse from the Bible with you...It's from Isaiah 41:10."

My family was in complete awe at this. Jeff then explained what had transpired the night before with the verse and Pastor Tim was equally astonished. Upon realizing that God was certainly sending a clear message he told Jeff, "Anything that has to do with God is NOT a coincidence."

-Jim

November 6th was an incredibly long and difficult day for our family. My father was scheduled for the kidney clamping early that morning. We were told the procedure would take a couple of hours and he would be in a great deal of pain when it was completed. The procedure was designed to aid in the reduction of blood loss during the removal of the kidney and tumor. Regardless of everything involved including the pain, it was a necessary step in the process.

While my father was having the delicate procedure done, my mother, sisters and I were in a waiting area nearby. We shared some of our nervous thoughts about the procedure, but were more concerned about the amount of pain he'd be in when it was finished. Our main hope was that they'd be able to control the pain and keep him comfortable.

We'd been waiting for awhile when one of the pastors from my church walked into the room. Pastor Tim Swanson had been aware and praying for of my father's situation for quite some time. I'd previously discussed when things would be taking place and he mentioned stopping by the hospital for a visit.

After making our way through introductions, we discussed the myriad of thoughts and worries we had. We talked about our concerns for the road ahead and what God had planned for my father. It felt good to have Tim there that morning, it was very comforting.

Eventually, Tim had other obligations to tend to and was preparing to leave. Before leaving, he asked if we'd like to join him in prayer and we agreed. He said, "Before we start I'd like to share a verse from the Bible with you...It's from Isaiah 41:10." I sat in total shock when he said those words. After fumbling through my words for a couple of seconds, I was finally able to explain what had happened with the verse the night before. Tim was equally surprised how God had revealed himself in such an awesome way.

After praying, Tim said his goodbyes and I walked with him to a nearby elevator. We continued to discuss the clear message that God was sending. Before boarding the elevator he said, "Anything that has to do with God is NOT a coincidence, He's telling us something here."

It was absolutely remarkable to see God working this way. None of us had experienced anything like it. Pastor Tim had no inclination of what had taken place the night before. There are thousands upon thousands of Bible verses, yet he felt compelled to share Isaiah 41:10. The exact verse our family had marveled at the evening before. God was definitely reaching out to us in unmistaken amazing way!

While walking back to the waiting area my thoughts turned to my own situation. Recent lab tests had alarmed my physician enough to schedule me with a hematologist for further evaluation. I couldn't help but wonder if I might also have cancer with my own difficult road ahead. My scheduled appointment was 5 days away, but there was simply too much going on with my father to be able to focus on my own needs. That day would come soon enough.

The surgeon finished with the kidney clamp procedure and my father was transported back to his room. The nurses and medical personnel took a few moments to check his vital signs while administering pain medication. Before entering his room, we were again reminded of the pain and discomfort he'd be experiencing. The medical staff reassured they'd do everything they could to keep him comfortable.

Upon entering the room it became very evident my father was in an extreme amount of pain. My mother, wife, two sisters and I, did our best to comfort him through words, and rubbing his arms and back. There were very few moments he appeared comfortable as wave after wave of pain would strike him. There was very little any of us could do and it left us with an incredibly helpless feeling to see him this way.

The day wore on as hours slowly crept by. The nurses attempted many times with different medications to alleviate his pain. At one point he'd grown very sick to his stomach which only made things worse. The emotional stress of seeing him like this had taken a toll on all of us. It was like living in a very bad dream.

Later that evening Pastor Tim stopped back in to see how my father was doing. I'd been finding it more and more difficult to see him in such pain and stepped out of the room with Tim. I did my best to keep my composure while telling him, "Now I'm beginning to understand what God must have felt watching His only Son Jesus dying on the cross." Watching my father suffer in pain through those difficult hours gave me a brief glimpse of how trying it must have been. What an incredible sacrifice it was!

Finally, after 10 hours of excruciating pain, the medical staff had found the right combination of medication to help him. The pain had subsided as well as the nausea. Seeing him finally resting comfortably put our minds at ease, if only for a moment. The operation to remove the kidney and tumor was scheduled for 7 a.m. the next day. As I walked out of his room that night, I couldn't help but wonder if we'd spent our last day on earth together.

Moments with God

"And the glory of the Lord will be revealed, and all mankind together will see it." –Isaiah 40:5

A few years back a movie titled "Evan Almighty" was released. The movie is a modern day version of Noah's ark. The main character Evan, played by the very funny Steve Carell, is approached by God, played so wonderfully by Morgan Freeman, to build an ark. The story takes many twists and turns as Evan tries desperately to avoid God. Evan finally gives up and obeys what God has commanded and he builds the ark.

It was only a movie, but if something like that actually happened it would be hard to imagine or believe. In fact, most people would react just as Evan's friends did and would think he was crazy. Many would try to distance themselves from the person very much like Evan's own family did. Fortunately for Evan, God had also revealed Himself to his wife convincing her that Evan was indeed sincere. After leaving for a short time, she returned with their children to help complete the building of the ark.

Wouldn't it be wonderful if God would reveal himself in such an open fashion in the hurting world we live in today? How different would things be if God routinely showed up at the White House to help with the key decisions being made each day? What would our world be like if He took part in NATO or other organizations that involve unity between global nations?

As wonderful as it would be to see the "physical" being of God, He continues to reveal Himself in many remarkable ways. The mere fact we are created in His own image is a revelation from God. I could go further and mention every living creature along with the air they breathe as examples of His revelation to us. God encompasses everything we are and know in our life on earth.

The greatest way God reveals Himself is through His word, the Bible. A prime example would be the unmistakable way He made His presence known through the events leading up to my father's surgery. The verse from which this book is titled, Isaiah 41:10, was God's unique way of revealing that He was near. It was a truly remarkable experience to have witnessed His presence and revelation to our family during those difficult days of 2008.

Prayer

Dear God, I praise You for revealing Yourself to me each and everyday. I pray that I might become more aware of Your subtle ways and to be bold in revealing Your good news to others. I thank You for Your blessings and for loving me for who I am. Amen.

11

CHAPTER

Saying Goodbye

Chapter 11
Saying Goodbye

Although I was heavily sedated the morning of my surgery, I was still well aware that most of my family was there to support me. They were also there to lean on each other through this emotional nightmare. Myself? I already knew what the outcome would be, God made it very clear to me in Isaiah.

I know this may be tough to understand, but I actually felt worse for my family and their worries than my own fears. I was numb over what was happening to me, but I also felt so alive. I was so filled by the Holy Spirit that I wanted to share it with everyone. I wanted so badly for everyone to take hold of the same peace I'd been experiencing.

As they prepared to wheel me into the operating room I was met with hugs from everyone that was there. I carried each one of those hugs and positive remarks with me into surgery. It was an incredible surreal moment.

Once in the room and moved onto the surgical table, the surgeons and nurses were all busy preparing me for the operation. I remember thinking to myself, "This could be the last chance I have to pray." I proceeded to call all of the surgeons and nurses to my side and I prayed for them. I have no memory of what I said. I just let God provide the words.

-Jim

It was after 1 a.m. before my sister's and I had left our father's room for the last time. We managed to find some semi-comfortable chairs in one of the surgical waiting areas of the hospital. We'd been so emotionally and physically drained a pile of bricks would have been comfortable to rest on.

My mother stayed with my father. I don't know how much sleep she was able to get, but I know things were beginning to really get tough for her. I'm sure much of the night was spent by his side holding his hand and recalling the many wonderful memories they'd shared through their many years together.

My sister's and I awoke sometime around 4:30 a.m. and made our way back to his room. The anxiety level I felt was immeasurable. I knew my father rested solely in God's hands and everything would happen according to His plan. A major part of me found it difficult to keep from feeling selfish and wanting him on earth awhile longer. I wasn't ready to let go, none of us were.

When we arrived, our mother was sitting bedside and our father was awake and resting comfortably. We greeted him with hugs and kisses and a few comments on how much better he looked from the day before. It was really remarkable he'd taken such a dramatic turn. It set the tone for what would be some wonderful yet difficult moments leading up to surgery.

During the next hour, before any other family members arrived, my father spent time talking with each one of us. He mentioned how much he loved and how proud he was of the kind of people we'd grown up to be. It was very difficult to keep composed during those moments. It wasn't long before the dams broke and the tears began to fall.

My brother Todd, who couldn't be released from his duties until the following day soon called. We listened as my father went through the same things he'd discussed with my sisters and me. As each minute passed it became harder and harder to face what was about to happen.

As time drew closer my father made a call to my house to talk with my children. It was very hard to listen to. Each one had their own special interests and he found a way to incorporate them into the conversation. Hearing him say goodbyes to my children was probably my toughest moment that morning. He then talked with my wife and shared some wonderful words with her.

Before long, we were joined by several other family members. In fact, the supporting cast was much too large to all fit into my father's room and spilled out into the hallway! The last moments spent in his room were filled with a few laughs but many tears.

Pastor Tim was also present that morning to pray with all of us before my father was taken to surgery. His prayer was an added strength our family desperately needed during those difficult moments. It was wonderful and very much appreciated.

When the transport team arrived to take my father to surgery I found myself desperately grasping for those last moments spent with him. I did my best to treasure everything said between us while suppressing the thought of losing him. I had floods of memories swirling through my mind as they wheeled him down the hall. I found myself trying to relive my lifetime spent with him in the few precious seconds we had left together.

After going down a few long halls we reached an elevator. It was very apparent the entire group wouldn't fit so my mother, two sisters and I rode with him. Amidst the fear that enveloped every inch of me, my father had a very calm sense of peace about him. What I witnessed in him was indescribable. It was clear to me that God's immeasurable love and comfort was cradling him all the way to the operating room.

My father went into a pre-surgery prep area for a short time before going into surgery. When our family was called over to say our final goodbyes we each shared one last moment with him. There were many hugs and tears as each person took their turn. When my time had arrived I approached him while doing my very best to keep things together. I leaned over and gave him a hug and kiss while whispering, "If you see the light run to it and don't look back...We'll be alright Dad, we'll be alright." My father told me he loved me and he'd be watching over my children.

After a few more goodbyes from family and friends it was time for him to go. Despite a few sniffles and dabbing of tears we all stood in silence while my father was wheeled away from us. I did my best treasure those last moments with him, but I became engulfed with thoughts of losing him. I looked up to see him being slowly wheeled now at a further distance. Before being pushed through the doors of the operating room he reached up for one last wave and then he was gone.

Moments with God

"While he was blessing them, he left them and was taken up to heaven." -Luke 24:51

It is very common for babies to go through a phase of separation anxiety. During the course of the first several months parents become the most recognizable persons and are very depended upon. They're the main provider of food, comfort, and protection, and are needed at all times.

Somewhere around the 9th or 10th month strangers become more recognizable. This is when separation anxiety really kicks into gear. The unshakable bond developed with parents can become threatened in the wake of being left with a face we're not accustomed to. When it so happens to take place, babies resort to crying out in vain while desperately reaching out to their parents to be picked up and carried away. Saying goodbyes just doesn't work out too well with separation anxiety.

It's very difficult to imagine what the disciples must have been going through leading up to Jesus' crucifixion. In reading the scriptures it becomes apparent there was confusion as to what was actually going to take place, along with moments of denial and deep despair. Jesus had called each of them to join Him in His ministry. Over the three years spent together He'd become their leader, friend, and brother. What would they do when He was gone?

Amidst the separation anxiety being felt within the group, Jesus spent time preparing them for what would be. There was much discussion around His prophesied persecution and death, along with what it would mean to the followers left behind. Jesus did His best to describe what would happen, but took great care in letting them know He'd be with them forever.

"Now is the time for judgment on this world, now the prince of this world will be driven out. But I, when I am lifted from this earth, will draw all men to myself." -John 12:31-32

Having to say goodbye was certainly not easy for the disciples of Jesus. Regardless of the amount of comfort they gained through the time spent before His crucifixion, they were human and had become emotionally invested in Him and His ministry. Saying goodbye when things had been going so well was not part their plans and was very difficult to deal with.

Through all of the imminent sorrow the disciples were facing Jesus continued to assure them. Jesus laid the groundwork for His resurrection.

"Now is your time for grief, but I will see you again and you will rejoice, and no one will take away your joy." -John 16:22

Through these words the disciples were being granted the opportunity to see Jesus again. It was a very difficult concept to grasp, but they took to heart His every word and believed.

In my final moments with my father before he was wheeled into surgery, I'd experienced many of the same emotions the disciples may have gone through. I wasn't prepared to lose my father and my own human nature caused my emotions to run rampant. It was a very difficult situation for me, my family, and everyone else near to him to face.

Despite the inherent fears we as humans face, Jesus' death on the cross has provided us with the same opportunities given to His followers so many years ago. We've also been granted the opportunity to one day see Jesus and be part of His eternal kingdom in heaven. Our time of grief will only be temporary, as will our life here on earth. One day we'll join the heavenly hosts to rejoice and sing praises to Him for all eternity.

Prayer

Dear God, thank You for sending Your son to die for me. I pray that I might continue to gain knowledge in Your word. As I continue to serve Your will for my life I pray that You will continue to fill me with Your Spirit. I love You my Lord and praise Your holy name. Amen.

CHAPTER 12

God's Miracle

Chapter 12
God's Miracle

I was heavily sedated at the time, but I can still vaguely remember my family's first visit with me in recovery. Amidst all of the different medications dripping into my arms I was aware enough to notice how everyone was filled with joy and happiness. They'd conveyed to me how the surgeon felt very confident everything had been removed and a full recovery looked very good.

The procedure involved the removal of my left kidney, adrenal gland, and the tumor that had infiltrated both areas. My heart was also by-passed to enable the surgeon to split the entire length of my vena cava (largest vein within the abdomen). They had to split my vena cava to scrape it's interior while reconstructing it. The tumor had grown inside of it and stretched it to twice the normal circumference. There were also 19 lymph nodes removed during the procedure which were sent for further testing. The final results of the testing revealed the lymph nodes and interior scrapings of the vena cava were all normal with no signs of cancer! PRAISE GOD FOR HIS MIRACLE IN MY LIFE!!

One of the resident physicians that had assisted with the procedure took time to pull Jeff aside and tell him, "There were more things going on in that operating room than what we were doing." He didn't elaborate and he didn't have to, Jeff knew...

Another awesome event happened that evening when my son-in-law brought their 3 daughters down to visit. Jeff began discussing the special things that had taken place around Isaiah 41:10. My oldest granddaughter Brooke was listening to the conversation and stood in astonishment. She proceeded to explain to everyone how she'd put Isaiah 41:10 on her cell phone just two weeks earlier. Once again God had revealed Himself in a magnificent way.

The mountain that stood before me with my cancer was one I couldn't climb alone. God not only blessed me with the strength to make it through, He communicated to us through His word. God was with us and making it very clear He wasn't leaving...

-Jim

I'd like to begin this chapter with a personal note of thanks and acknowledgement to everyone who took the time to be with our family during my father's surgery. There were aunts, uncles, cousins, pastors, and friends who were supportive through those difficult long hours of waiting. The time spent with you that day visiting, praying, laughing, and crying will never be forgotten. Our family will be forever grateful for the love you shared. It was a true blessing for all of us.

After my father was wheeled into surgery, our entourage entered into a waiting area adjacent to the operating room. I remember seeing several other people scattered amongst the chairs throughout the spacious room. As we each found a seat I began to reflect on the magnitude of what was taking place. Did I just say goodbye to my father for the last time? If he made it through surgery what was the chance that the cancer had spread to other areas of his body?

The previous days and months had been long and arduous, but none compared to November 7, 2008. Shortly after we'd entered the waiting area, we were informed periodic calls would be made from the operating room to update us on how things were progressing. We found this very helpful, but also nerve racking. Every time the phone rang ears perked up, necks strained, and all eyes focused towards the staff person who'd answered the phone. This went on for the first couple of hours before we'd received our first update. He was stable and the operation was going as planned. A sense of relief could be felt through the room. It was really great to have received one of the first pieces of good news in months.

The minutes and hours continued to slowly creep by and the clock showed it was nearing noon. I hadn't had much of an appetite, but as different groups began leaving for lunch my wife convinced me to get something to eat. My good friend Scott, who'd been waiting with me and my family, joined us on our lunch excursion. The search wasn't long before we located a small café next door to the hospital. The busy quaint restaurant offered a nice variety of soups and deli sandwiches to go along with its warm atmosphere. The food was fairly priced and very good. It proved to be an excellent decision by the three of us.

I found the time spent away from everything to be the break I really needed, not only for nourishment, but also my mental state of mind. I'd been inside the hospital since the wee hours of the day before and the minor reprieve was nice. It allowed me to escape the heaviness and stress laden waiting area, giving me the opportunity to catch my breath before facing the unknown conclusion to my father's surgery.

Upon our return to the hospital, we were greeted by everyone that had either made their way back from lunch, or hadn't left at all. Over the next several hours I'd noticed a growing anticipation and inescapable weariness begin to envelope all who were waiting. It was really getting mentally tough, but God continued to bless us with more unexpected visits from friends, relatives, and pastors. Through these people we became surrounded by God's love. It became the strength our family desperately needed to endure the long wait.

It was going on 4 p.m. before we'd finally received word the surgery was completed and my father was in recovery. We were also informed at that time the surgeon would be meeting with our family in a conference room adjacent to the waiting area. There was a true sense of relief when we'd realized he'd made it through the surgery, but whether it was successful or not remained unknown.

My mother, two sisters and I, were joined by our spouses in the conference room. A few other family members which included my mother's sister, Ruth, and my father's brother, Mark, joined us as well. The wait wasn't long before the visibly exhausted surgeon came through the door. A very calm look took shape as he sat at a seat across from us. His soft spoken voice matched his demeanor when he said the words, "The operation was successful and I believe we got it all." An explosion of tears, hugs, and cries of joy filled the small room. The surgeon was very humble and paused for a moment before going into further detail. He mentioned there was no visible evidence the cancer had spread and 19 lymph nodes were removed to be tested. They'd visibly appeared normal, but needed to be looked at with more detail. Before leaving the room my mother stood and gave him a big hug. As tears streamed down her face she thanked him for giving my father a second chance.

The celebration of God's miracle poured out of the small conference room and into the waiting area. The rest of our family and friends had been anxiously waiting us. The same shouts of joy and tears flowed freely as we shared the awesome news. It wasn't long before the miraculous news made its way through the throngs of curious bystanders. Many of them were awaiting the fate of their own loved ones, but were happy to join in our celebration.

My father spent the next hour in recovery before being transported to a surgical intensive care unit. I cannot remember the precise moment, but at one point I crossed paths with one of the other surgeons that had assisted with the lengthy operation. I took the opportunity to thank him for being part of the team, but the most powerful part of our conversation was what he shared with me. He said, "There was more going on in that room than what we were doing." He didn't elaborate anymore on the statement and I didn't say anything back to him. We simply looked at each other and smiled both realizing we'd been a part of something very special. We, and everyone else present that day, had experienced the miraculous healing touch of God.

Three days later...

It had been nearly a week since I'd received news about my blood work. My appointment with the hematologist was now only a day away and my anxieties had grown tenfold. As my father continued to fight his way toward recovery my focus began to turn toward my own situation.

As I prepared to go to bed that night I knew I wouldn't sleep. The stress of my father's situation and my own had taken its toll on me. I'd honestly become an emotional train wreck and had grown desperate for just an ounce of peace.

Before climbing into bed I decided to search for comfort in God's word. I turned to Isaiah 41:10 and read over it a few times before lying down next to my wife. While clutching the Bible tightly against my chest, I closed my eyes and began to plead in silent prayer. When I finished I glanced over at my wife and watched her peacefully sleep.

With tears streaming down my cheeks I whispered, "I can't leave her now Lord, I can't leave her now."

I continued to battle the restlessness for a couple more hours before surrendering and climbing out of bed. I decided perhaps a change of scenery might help so I made my way into our youngest son Brenner's room. He'd fallen asleep in his brother Brock's room so his bed was empty. Before climbing into the bed I decided to once again go to God in prayer. I searched and stumbled over many words before an old familiar verse came to mind, "Be still and know that I am God."

I was on my knees clutching my Bible in my hands as I recited the verse over and over. I was physically and emotionally exhausted and rested my head down onto the bed. I remember taking notice of the silence, everything was absolutely still. As I continued to whisper the verse something extraordinary happened. A sudden and very vivid vision crossed into my mind. I was on my knees and at the feet of the Lord with my head resting in His lap and He was gently caressing my head. I then felt a wave of overwhelming peace that enveloped the entire room. I'd never felt so close to God in all my life. It was a surreal and incredible experience that words will never fully be able to describe.

The rest of my night went well as God blessed me with an abundant sense of peace. After seeing our children off to school the next morning, my wife and I made the short drive to the cancer center for my appointment. Upon entering the facility, I was directed to a lab area to have my blood drawn. The blood was processed immediately and after a short wait I was taken to an examination room to meet with the hematologist.

The first order of business was to go over the results of the blood tests. The hematologist was a very kind middle-aged man who calmly smiled when he revealed that everything looked normal. He remained calm but I nearly collapsed to the floor with relief. It was as if the weight of the world had been lifted from my shoulders. The hematologist then went through a thorough medical history and examination of me before deciding I was healthy and there was nothing more he'd recommend.

When we exited the office I took Valerie in my arms and just wept. It was a total outpouring of emotions from the day and past week. I'd become emotionally drained, but I was also extremely overwhelmed by God's grace and mercy.

Moments with God

"God also testified to it by signs, wonders and various miracles, and gifts of the Holy Spirit distributed according to his will."

-Hebrews 2:4

As I read this passage from Paul found in Hebrews I began to reflect upon the journey our family went through in 2008. The difficult journey had as many shocking and unexpected turns as a big screen thriller, but God would not be outdone. He provided us with many wondrous signs and a miracle that has changed many lives. He met us in our desperate time of need and never left our side.

There are a couple of key elements in Hebrews 2:4 that we should take note of. First is the fact that God used, *"signs, wonders, and various miracles, and gifts of the Holy Spirit"* to testify to people. From Genesis to Revelations the Bible has a plethora of signs and miracles from God. These were key elements of communication and testifying His reigning almighty power.

The good news for us today is the fact we share the same God and He communicates in the very same way. A prime example is my father's miraculous journey with cancer. God communicated to our family through a sign in Isaiah 41:10 and He testified to us through the miracle He provided with my father's surgery. He let us know He was near and would uphold us through everything. People, I'm here to tell you, "We serve a living God!" The God of Abraham and Isaac so many years ago is the same God for you and me today.

The last part of Hebrews 2:4 is the most telling part of the entire verse. God does everything *"according to his will."* Every sign, wondrous act, and miracle is done according to His will. This also holds true for us today. Each one of God's blessings bestowed upon us is done according to His will.

This all sounds great and we can praise Him in thanksgiving, but there is a downside and it goes something like this. What we want and what God wants for us don't always line up together. Sometimes we wonder if they ever do! My father's miraculous bout with cancer could have ended in a much different way if it was God's will. God could have chosen to lead our family to Isaiah 41:10 to give us a sign He was near, but not allow the miraculous surgery to take place. This is an easy concept to comprehend, but it's not always easy to accept. It's my firm belief this mystery is one of many to be revealed when we enter the gates of heaven.

So what can we take from all of this? God will continue to testify through miracles and wondrous signs, and as followers of Christ we need to be vigilant and watch for them. When we are blessed to have experienced or witnessed one of God's amazing works we must be willing to share the good news with everyone. If God is willing to provide moments of grace and mercy in our lives we must be willing to share the good news of the provision.

Prayer

Heavenly Father, I come to You with thanksgiving and praise today. Your wondrous signs and miracles do not go unnoticed. Your awesome power and will is not mistaken. Help me to have the strength and courage to share Your wondrous deeds in my life. Guide me with the words to say to speak Your good news to everyone.

CHAPTER

13

Guidance

Chapter 13
Guidance

When I first received news I had cancer I became very humble with my life and the possibility of death. I turned all of my feelings of fear and uncertainty over to God. His promise in the Bible of "always being there" allowed me to seek His guidance through my entire ordeal. I then found myself having more open conversations with my Lord then ever before.

-Jim

There's much to be said about summer mornings. Hearing birds singing high in the trees as the sun gently awakes the world always sets a tone for another great day. It was the summer of 1973, and I was a happy young 5 year old living life without a care in the world. Although I don't remember the exact day it happened, the event lives in my mind as if it was yesterday.

Earlier that spring my mother and father had surprised me with my first bicycle. It was purple with white trim and really looked big compared to the tricycle I'd grown accustomed to. Although intimidating at first, I grew to love the wonderful machine and felt great riding it. I spent countless hours pedaling around with the air whistling through my ears while the clangs and pings of training wheels followed close behind.

On this particular day, I'd decided it was time to get the taste of total freedom by having the training wheels removed. I was ready for the challenge! After some good coaxing on my part I was able to get my father to agree and I think he was as excited as I was. After a few turns of a wrench my father smiled at me before setting the wheels aside.

Now, when most children learn to ride without training wheels it's usually by pedaling down a driveway, cul-de-sac, or along a sidewalk while being guided by the person teaching them to ride. The scene has played out countless times on television or in movies. A mother or father is gently guiding a child along while holding onto the back of the seat. The child continues to pedal as the mother or father gently lets go. The scene concludes with the mother or father raising their arms in joyous celebration while the child wobbles along smiling ear to ear. What a wonderful moment for everyone!

My shining moment without training wheels was a little more unorthodox than the Hallmark commercial I just described. Let's just say my father's methods were a little bit different. We've all become familiar with the large aircraft carriers that play such an important role in the United States Navy. They are occupied and operated by some of our nations finest, some of which include pilots. These brave men and women climb into fighter jets which are launched from the flight deck over open waters below. These people carry an unbelievable amount of trust and confidence in each other, but exhibit a tremendous amount of courage and bravery as well.

On the day my father taught me how to ride without training wheels I caught a glimpse of what it must be like being launched from one of those carriers. No, I wasn't actually being launched from one of them, but for a 5 year old kid it was equally as exhilarating.

As I climbed onto the seat my father steadied the bicycle in an upright position. I firmly gripped the handlebars and felt the excitement begin to build. Ahead of me was 15 feet of sidewalk that came to an abrupt halt as it met the lush green grass of our backyard. As the butterflies began fluttering in my stomach my father took hold of the seat.

"Are you ready?" he asked with a grin on his face.

"Yeah," I replied without the slightest hesitation.

There was a sudden jolt and I was soon traveling forward. My little feet were crazily spinning as my legs attempted to keep up with the speed at which I was traveling. When we reached the end of the sidewalk, my father gave me one last heave. In an instant I'd become just like one of those fighter pilots sailing across the sea.

"Pedal! Pedal! Pedal!!" called out my father.

Pedal I did, and it was with everything I had. After traveling about 30 to 40 feet I eventually slowed and tipped onto the ground. Not far behind was my father giving words of encouragement as he helped me back up.

There were many other subsequent launches from the USS Yosick sidewalk. Each launch ended with me tipping over somewhere in the yard, but each time I'd traveled a bit further. Regardless of how well I did each time my father was there to pick me up, dust me off, and guide me back onto the bike again.

I was eventually able to maintain my balance enough to graduate to the driveway and other sidewalks flying solo. None of this would have ever been possible without the guiding hands and encouragement by my father.

Moments with God

"The Lord will guide you always; he will satisfy your needs in a sun-scorched land and will strengthen your frame. You will be like a well-watered garden, like a spring whose waters never fail."

- Isaiah 58:11

Just as my father's hands were guiding me on the journey of learning to ride a bicycle, God's hands are continually guiding us along as we pass each day here on earth. We can't always see or feel them, but they are always there continuously guiding.

When I think about guidance I'm quickly drawn to one of my father's favorite chapters in the Bible which is Psalm 23.

"The Lord is my shepherd; I shall not be in want. He makes me lie down in green pastures, He leads me beside quiet waters, he restores my soul. He guides me in paths of righteousness for his name's sake. Even though I walk through the valley of the shadow of death, I will fear no evil, for you are with me. Your rod and your staff, they comfort me. You prepare a table for me in the presence of my enemies.

You anoint my head with oil; my cup overflows. Surely goodness and love will follow me all the days of my life, and I will dwell in the house of the Lord forever."

This particular passage reflects upon the nature of the Lord as a shepherd. It describes how He leads and guides us with His rod and staff, very much as a shepherd would lead his sheep. Psalm 23 explains this guidance as a comfort in our time of need and how it keeps us on the path of righteousness. God's presence within this passage is as real for us today as it was for David centuries ago.

When God created this wonderful world we live in He filled it with people of all different colors, cultures, climates, and nations. We were all created very diverse and unique, but we will all experience hardships in life. This could range from being born with a handicap, being stricken with a major illness or dealing with the death of someone close. There may be endless days of sleepless nights where we find ourselves waiting for God to intervene. Where are you God? Why have you let this happen to me?

These very same questions were asked by Jesus as he hung on the cross. *"My God, my God, why have you forsaken me?"* (Matthew 27:46). Jesus was a living breathing human being. He was fulfilling God's will for Him on earth, yet in His darkest hour of hardship questioned why God had forsaken Him. Where are you Father? Why must I die on this cross?

We'll never fully comprehend God's will in our lives, but one thing is certain, He's always there guiding us through each hardship we face. God's guidance will lead us to the strength, wisdom, and courage needed to make it through. It may not be as noticeable as the sign He provided for our family in Isaiah 41:10, but He will be the guide to see us through. Just as my father guided me along with my bicycle, our Shepherd is along side of us with a staff in hand to guide us throughout our lives.

Prayer

Heavenly Father, please renew my soul today with an understanding that You are my guide. I realize that there will be many happy times in my life, but there will also be some hardships that will be difficult to face. I pray that I will continue to feel Your guidance throughout my life and will never forget that You'll forever be there through every day. Amen.

CHAPTER

14

Giving of Ourselves

Chapter 14
Giving of Ourselves

Shortly after the shock of hearing the news of my cancer diagnosis, I turned and offered myself to God...mind and body. He was the only one that could heal me. How much would you give to save your life?

-Jim

I grew up with a passion for sports. I'm not honestly sure where it all began for me, but if it involved a ball, it had my full attention. Regardless of its roots my passion for sports has lasted my entire life. In fact, I would go as far to say I'd find this world very boring if I didn't have the opportunity to follow and to cheer for my favorite teams.

My father helped fuel my thirst for sports at a young age. Together we spent countless hours throwing the football, or playing catch with the baseball. I can vividly remember this special time together occurring mostly after dinner. He worked third shift back then and would get his rest through the morning and early afternoon. Regardless of how tough the night before had been, or how much rest he had gotten that morning, he was always willing to make time for me. If he hadn't been so giving of his time, I probably wouldn't have developed such a love for sports.

My first taste of playing an organized sport was on the baseball diamond. I was seven at the time and was so small in stature that swinging the lightest bat available was a monumental task for me. I took over my father's retired softball glove which literally reached below my knees when it was held against my waste. The old glove stayed with me throughout all of my baseball playing days, and I still have it today.

My father spent time coaching the various baseball teams I'd played on and it was a great experience having him as a coach. Although I was his son, I never felt like I had any special treatment. All of the other players were taught to play a sport we'd all loved by a man willing to give of himself and his time. Not to mention the fact he loved doing it. He treated and coached each one of us with the same dignity, love, and respect. He cared about each individual.

When I was thirteen, I was playing for one of the teams my father had coached. The league consisted of two teams from our hometown along with others across the county. It was referred to as the "traveling team league" consisting mainly of 12 and 13 year old kids. Playing on one of these teams was an ultimate goal for many of the younger players.

Like most baseball leagues amateur or professional, the regular season ended with a tournament. The nice thing about this league was the fact every team was entered into the tournament regardless of their regular season record. It gave each team a chance to end the season on a high note.

During the tournament of my final year in the league I was pitching in one of the semi-final games. I really loved to pitch. I was never an overpowering pitcher, but through some great tutelage from my father I became decent. My best pitch was the curveball. It was very difficult for me to throw it when first taught, but over time I was able to really get the ball to hook across the plate.

In this particular game, both teams were one win away from playing for the championship. Both were very good and carrying quite a bit of momentum going in. It was actually one of the most important games any of us had ever played in.

I was really off to a great start that day. My control was good and was I having some success with the curveball. I'd given up a few hits, but for the most part, the batters were having some difficulty hitting my pitches. The game progressed with our team jumping out to an early lead. I continued to pitch with efficiency as one of the opposing team's star players stepped to the plate. It was a pivotal moment in the game and I had two strikes on this player. I wound up to throw my next pitch and released it. As the ball reached the plate area the batter jumped back away from it before it gently dove across the plate into the catcher's mitt.

"Strike three!" shouted the umpire.

It was one of the best curveballs I'd ever thrown. Within seconds of the umpire uttering those wonderful words the coach of the opposing team came running toward the plate.

"He can't throw that pitch! It's against the rules!" he shouted.

What I thought was going to be something great was quickly turning into something very ugly. Upon seeing things begin to unfold, my father came out onto the field toward the umpire and other coach. The discussion was heated and almost surreal. A few minutes had passed before the umpire pulled the rule book out and began pouring through it. During this time my father had made his way out to the mound where I was standing.

I'd become visibly shaken from the ordeal and my father could see it. In that very instant he was no longer a coach, but a father doing his best to console his child. He tried to explain what was happening, but the most important thing he did was to tell me to not let what was happening bother me. I did my best to keep myself focused, but continued to find it difficult to keep my composure.

After several minutes of delaying the game the umpire called the coaches to home plate for a short meeting. In his search of the rule book the umpire found nothing related to the use of a curveball in little league play. My father and the other coach returned to their respective benches and the game resumed.

By that time I'd become a bundle of emotions. I was distraught at what had just transpired, but even more upset because there was no rule against what I was doing. The coach for the other team was unsuccessful with the umpire and rule book, but victorious in affecting the rest of my performance.

As my concentration and emotions unraveled, I totally stopped throwing the curveball and only threw fastballs. It wasn't long before my overall control over my pitches had diminished. When I did get one across the plate the other team feasted on it. The lead we had quickly evaporated into a humiliating loss.

The key to this entire story isn't about losing a game, but due to the willingness of my father to be a coach he was able to be there for me in a special way. I needed more than just a coach to tell me to keep my chin up during those circumstances. Having him there meant the world to me, especially that day.

We shared many wonderful moments and won quite a few games together throughout my years of playing baseball, but that day in particular will remain the most memorable for me. My father had successfully taught me the value of always being willing to give of myself, and when to take the coach's cap off and be a father.

Moments with God

"Give and it will given to you. A good measure, pressed down,
shaken together and running over, will be poured into your lap."

-Luke 6:38

One of the greatest examples of giving of oneself was Jesus. Sent as a gift for all of mankind, Jesus spent his entire ministry giving to others. From time spent with the sick and hurting, to His final breath on the cross, Jesus gave.

Throughout each of our daily lives we're exposed to countless opportunities to give of ourselves. For many people things become so busy that trying to fit one more item on our schedule could tip the scale of what was almost manageable. Regardless of the circumstances, these opportunities will continue to be there as long as time exists.

When I read the Bible and reflect upon the life and ministry of Jesus, I've come to realize much of His time was dedicated to what would be considered the outcasts of society. Jesus spent time counseling and healing lepers, tax collectors, and prostitutes. He willingly shared His ministry to all who wanted to listen, but much of what was recorded in scripture was with those less fortunate. So what was God trying to convey through all of this? If Jesus was really a king, then why wasn't He spending time with royalty?

It is my humble opinion that the love and compassion Jesus shared with the hurting world around Him should be viewed as God's living lesson for us. The goal of all followers of Christ should be based on a life where time and resources are focused on the hurting and less fortunate. These resources go beyond giving monetarily, but more importantly includes the giving of ourselves and time.

Mother Theresa was a wonderful example of living life in the mold of our Savior Jesus during her time here on earth. Most of her adult years were spent caring for those in need in some of the most impoverished locations on earth. Many were sick and dying from famine and disease with a greater population of them being children.

Mother Theresa wrote a poem I'm very fond of titled, "Be Nice Anyway." It's a very straight forward, to the point poem I keep hanging in my office. One particular line of the poem reads:

"Give the world the best you have, and it may not be enough.
Give the world the best you've got anyway."
-Mother Theresa

What a powerful statement from such a humble human being. Because of the kind of life she lived, it's impossible for me to believe she was solely referring to monetary gifts. Rather, Mother Theresa was speaking directly about the willingness to give of ourselves to the needs of others. The giving of our time, compassion, love and empathy wherever and whenever it's needed. Acting upon this wonderful example of God's own unconditional love for us is a direct reflection of His only Son's selfless life on earth.

I was fortunate to have been raised in a home with two wonderful examples of self giving in my mother and father. I consider it both a challenge and responsibility to be the same kind of example to my three children, and carry a hope that one day they'll do the same.

Prayer

Father God, I come to You with thanksgiving in my heart. I praise You for Your only Son Jesus and for the example He was here on earth. Help me to look beyond the business of my day and allow me to see the world through Your eyes. Help me to be more giving of myself through not only my actions, but also my words. I give You thanks and praise for this day and this moment. Amen.

CHAPTER

15

Encouragement

Chapter 15
Encouragement

There were so many things God did to bless me with encouragement, one being my family. One of the questions I thought about often was based on how my family would go on without me. It was difficult at times to find total comfort with those thoughts. The ties that bind us are so painfully strong in such difficult times. God blessed me with a comfort and peace through those moments by being present with me along each difficult step of my journey.

-Jim

When one looks at the word "encouragement" it doesn't take long to realize the word "courage" sits smack dab in the middle. So the act of giving someone encouragement is actually helping the person muster up "courage" to conquer whatever it is they're facing. Encouragement is truly the main component to most of the success that's ever achieved. In fact, many people who were ready to throw in the towel and give up on a job, invention, or even a relationship, found the "courage" to press on from a simple gesture of encouragement. Very much like a plant needs water and sunshine we need encouragement.

Both my mother and father were never short on encouragement. I experienced quite a bit of it while growing up and it continues today. This encouragement dates back to my first few steps of walking without them holding my hand through the rest of my days as a child and adolescent. Today their encouragement comes as I face all of the trials and tribulations of fatherhood.

Encouragement has been that little extra boost when I've really needed it. It's picked me up through some tough times and kept me moving forward when I've been ready to quit. I'll never underestimate what the impact of encouragement from my parents has done for me. I do know I'll be forever thankful for every ounce of it.

My father had some very unique quotes I was privileged to hear while growing up. For those that truly know him, you know exactly what I'm talking about! Many were used as a form of encouragement and there are many I could share. One of my favorite's was a simple phrase I heard over and over, "If you give half the effort, you'll get half the results."

What a wonderful and easy to comprehend piece of information. In fact, now that I know it's actually true I've found myself using the exact words with my own children. My father really liked to use this line when he knew I was slacking and not giving it my all. There was usually enough firmness in the tone of his voice as he delivered the words to get my attention, and it was usually successful. As much as I would like to claim I gave 110% at everything I did, I cannot. There were far too many instances I heard this line to claim I always gave 110%. It was, however, very successful with persuading me to make the needed adjustments in the effort I was giving.

The other story on encouragement I'd like to share is truly one of my favorites. I played football while in high school, and before each Friday evening game I'd have dinner with my family. When it was time to leave the house my father would always utter the phrase, "Break a leg." I'm not sure of the origin of the phrase, but I know it's another way to wish someone luck.

I was a junior in high school and my position on the team was quarterback that year. I wasn't very big, about 5'8 and weighing about 155 pounds soaking wet. Needless to say, it made my mother a little nervous seeing me take some of the hits from opposing players during games. This particular night left plenty for her to be nervous about.

We were playing against our rival school and it was the second half of the game. Both teams were really battling on the field. We had possession of the ball and I was dropping back to throw a pass. Before I was able to release it I was hit very hard from behind. As I was crumpling to the ground I severely twisted my left ankle. I'd never experienced a pain quite like that before. I'd been through ankle sprains, but this one felt very different.

Once I was scraped off the field and taken to the sideline, a physician from town took a look at my ankle. My mother and father soon joined us on the sideline as well. My pain was very intense, but I was much more concerned about what the doctor would say.

"It looks like you've broken your leg," were his exact words.

Yes, that's right! The doctor said that my leg was broken. I couldn't believe it! My father's wonderful words of encouragement had finally soaked in. I went and broke my leg!

The doctor suggested getting my leg x-rayed in his office after the game just to be sure. The x-rays revealed my leg wasn't broken after all. However, there were some ligaments that were damaged which forced me to miss the final three games of the season. Although my father meant nothing but good things through encouraging words, he never said them to me again.

The whole incident reminded me of the movie "A Christmas Story." The main character Ralphie wanted a BB gun for Christmas but was told over and over, "You'll shoot your eye out, kid." Ralphie shrugged this notion off and indeed received this BB gun he so desperately wanted. He was given the green light to shoot it for the first time only to see the prophecy come true. "Oh no, I shot my eye out!" The BB had ricocheted back and hit him squarely in the eye. Thankfully for Ralphie, his eyes were protected from the trusty glasses. He hadn't shot his eye out after all!

I truly wouldn't have attained any of the success I've tasted in life without sound encouragement from my parents. Their encouragement ranged from cheering me on during games when I was younger, to something very subtle such as words written in a birthday cards I still receive today. Regardless, their encouragement will always remain as a key stepping stone to my successes in life.

Moments with God

"But encourage one another daily." – Hebrews 3:13

We live in a society today in which we've become very accustomed to the notion of self-reliance. In fact, it's something most of us are taught from a young age until we're old enough to leave the nest. When we leave some of us go off to college while others become employed within the workforce. Eventually, according to the "American dream," we get married have a couple of kids and buy the three bedroom home down the street.

These things are all obtained through hard work, dedication and being successful with the goals we set. However, none of it can be accomplished without encouragement from those we share relationships with along the way. Whether it's a brother, pastor, teacher, parent, or friend, if they've encouraged us they've become an ingredient to our success.

Just as we've utilized our relationships here on earth to encourage each other throughout our lives, Paul, the author of Hebrews, is calling on us to encourage each other in a different way.

Paul calls on people to come together and form relationships which will encourage each other along our spiritual journey. We must learn to form and foster positive relationships that can be counted on through each of our struggles and all of our joys. When these types of spiritual relationships are developed, it allows us to step into a totally different level of understanding together. Through time, prayer, and trust, this type of relationship can produce accountability. When we're in a relationship where accountability is considered the foundation, our daily struggles with sin and worldly ways become easier to conquer.

If you've struggled to find a relationship like this in your life, earnestly seek through prayer for God to intervene and perhaps provide someone that could possibly be searching for the same thing. Developing a trusting relationship may take time. However, in the end, encouraging each other to be accountable will be a key to your successful walk as a Christian.

Prayer

Dear God, please help me to be more encouraging to those around me. Fill me with an understanding and wisdom of what true encouragement means. I long for relationships with those who carry the same values as I. Please guide me to find and to foster relationships that would encourage me to remain accountable in all that I do and say. Amen.

CHAPTER 16

Faithfulness

Chapter 16
Faithfulness

"Faithfulness is all that God asks of us. I never lost faith through my bout with cancer. In fact, it only grew. Good or bad I've always felt that God wants what's best for us. Whether my outcome ended with good news or bad, I was ready to accept what He had in store for me."

-Jim

It's my humble opinion that faithfulness should be considered as one of the most powerful words in the English language. I say this because faith is the very foundation in which our relationship with God and each other is founded and sustained. Without faithfulness relationships would cease to exist.

In our relationship with God we must first develop a faith and belief He indeed exists. As our faith in Him continues to blossom we come to the realization He's always abiding with us and taking care of our needs. In turn, we become faithful to Him through the way we live out our daily lives. We begin to live lives according to the Bible, lives which are holy and pleasing to God.

These same principles of faith are a direct reflection of our relationships with others, especially our spouses. Just as faith is a key component to our relationship with God, faithfulness is essential to the foundation of marriage. The faithfulness shared in a relationship between a man and woman can become an unshakeable force when it's based on the model faith between man and God.

My parents will be celebrating their 44th wedding anniversary this year. I couldn't have had a better demonstration of faithfulness to learn from. The love and devotion between them has continued to grow stronger as each year passes. Our entire family has been fortunate enough to witness firsthand how they've stuck together through both good times and bad. This bond couldn't have been more evident six years ago.

It was a typical November day in 2004 when the phone rang in my office. Most of my thoughts were on the upcoming feast of Thanksgiving and time spent with family sharing laughs and great food. The thoughts of the wonderful days ahead were soon dashed by the tone of my mother's voice at the end of the line.

My mother had recently had a mammogram that had shown a suspicious area in her breast. The doctors decided she should have a biopsy performed. "Jeff, the results weren't good," was all she needed to say. As a lump slowly formed in the base of my throat I scrambled for whatever words I could respond with, I quickly entered a state of denial. The only thought racing through my brain was, "This isn't real. These things just don't happen to us." The conversation changed into a discussion on what would happen next and the plans of treatment the physician had recommended. What I'd hoped was only a bad dream suddenly became something very real, my mother had been diagnosed with breast cancer.

The news for our family couldn't have come at a more difficult time. My brother Todd, who serves in the Army, was nearing the end of his 10th month in Iraq. It had been a very difficult load for all of us, especially my parents. The latest news would make for a very difficult holiday season for our entire family.

When the holidays arrived there were some tough moments, but we made it through. There was still the glow in the eyes of the grandchildren, and we'd enjoyed time together while sharing memories of Christmas past. With my brother serving in Iraq and the mountain my mother was facing, there was a distinct somberness in the air which couldn't be avoided.

My mother's surgery was completed during the first week of January and was successful without any complications. The next several months were spent going from one appointment to another as she slowly recovered while battling the disease. The process became a real roller coaster ride for my mother, full of ups and downs in the way she felt physically and mentally.

I'll never be able to fully express the gratitude I have for my parents for the unspoken life lessons taught to me through those difficult days. In my father I saw the words "in sickness and in health" being lived out before my very eyes. Although I know that this was tough on him, my father was a rock through everything, never leaving my mother's side.

It's hard to believe they reversed their roles for each other only a few years later with my father's bout with cancer. They've both shown me what being faithful to a commitment meant, and when we're fortunate to have found someone to spend our lives with it must be nurtured and cherished through good times and bad.

In my mother's bout with cancer I saw in her an inner strength which could only be described as someone truly living on faith, and a belief this faith would see her through. When some of us grew weak along her journey she always remained positive and strong. My mother had become a hero for all of us and I'll always treasure the living example of what true faith is.

It was through my mother's battle that I became inspired to write "Running the Race," a children's book based around breast cancer. It's my sincere hope the book will serve as an educational tool for children of loved ones stricken with this disease to help them to better understand and cope with such a difficult time.

The faithfulness I've witnessed in both my father and mother through their bouts with cancer is something I'll always cherish. They remained faithful to their relationship between each other, but more importantly they relied on their faith in God through the difficult roads. If I'm able to carry a fraction of the love and faithfulness I've witnessed between my parents I'd die a very blessed man.

Moments with God

"Let love and faithfulness never leave you; bind them around your neck, write them on the tablet of your heart." –Proverbs 3:3

As one spends any amount of time in the Bible, it doesn't take very long to realize there is a long historical relationship between God and man. It becomes very evident throughout the Old Testament with great men such as Adam, Moses, Abraham, Isaac, and the prophets. It continues directly into the New Testament with God's only Son Jesus and His disciples. All throughout the Bible there is a direct connection between God and man. One of the biggest components of maintaining this relationship was faith.

This same connection with God continues to be available for us today. Through the death and resurrection of His only Son Jesus, we've been granted a clear and direct relationship with God. The same God faithful in bringing Moses and the Israelites through the desert is the same God faithful to our needs today.

As our love and faithfulness goes with God, so does our love and faithfulness with each other. The correlation is uncanny, yet true. It is very difficult to maintain healthy relationships without the ultimate model of faith between God and man. Our success as Christians will be measured by what we do with our faith. We must not allow our faith to become stagnate and withering in the sun. Faith is something to be nurtured each day and must become the very fabric of who we are. Faith must always remain the cornerstone of our daily lives.

Prayer

Heavenly Father, I thank and praise You for Your faithfulness to me. Please continue to fill me with the wisdom and strength to remain faithful in my relationship with You and others. I praise You for sending Your Son Jesus Christ to die so that I might one day live. He was a living beacon of Your faithfulness for all of mankind and I thank you for Him. Amen.

CHAPTER 17

Patience

Chapter 17
Patience

We as humans are very impatient. If we have a thorn in our finger we want it immediately removed. If we are suffering from a cold or seasonal flu we can hardly wait to begin to feel better. I was stricken with a tumor the size of a Nerf football in me, and yes, I wanted it out now!

Through God's guidance, the physicians put me on a medication to slow the progression of the tumor. The medication made me very weak and caused a few other side effects, but the hardest part was how painfully slow it was. Amidst all of the side effects and time spent wondering if I'd truly make it, God filled me with a peaceful assurance things would be alright. I simply needed to rely on Him and be patient. Throughout my ordeal I found it was much easier and important to pray for understanding. The patience, in turn, became a product of my understanding.

-Jim

Almost everyone has heard the phrase, "patience is a virtue" at one time or another. As true as the statement is, we live in a society that teaches us the direct opposite. There are 24 hour stores and fast food chains, we can catch the news during any part of the day, and we literally have the entire world at our fingertips with the internet. Being surrounded by all of these wonderful things has made patience a less important commodity.

If you've been fortunate enough to have been blessed with children, then at some point you've come to the realization of how patience is a key to survival. Having patience is an essential tool in the art of raising children. Unfortunately, some people, including myself, can find patience to be a very difficult thing to obtain. Even people who consider patience as one of their strongest virtues can fall into lapses of patience.

Being a parent is certainly not a job for wimps. In fact, I've heard remarks in certain circles how parenting is considered life's most difficult occupation. Going into our 13th year as parents my wife and I are finding out how true this statement is. There are many occupations considered to be more physically and emotionally demanding, but none carry the amount of responsibility parenthood does. Parents are responsible for the care and livelihood of another human being. Providing for and raising them into what will hopefully one day be good citizens whom love and respect others.

My parents were blessed with four children. Being the oldest I've often labeled myself as "the guinea pig." This is a term most often associated with the first born or oldest child. Let's be honest, parents can't fully understand everything about parenthood until they've gained experience by becoming one. This is where all of the experimental testing on the firstborn or should I say "guinea pig" takes place. I like to think my testing must have gone fairly well considering the fact three siblings came along after me!

All kidding aside, I was truly a key training ground for the development of my parent's patience. It was me that dirtied those first diapers and went through the temper tantrums of the terrible twos. It was me that broke the beautiful ceramic heirlooms passed down to my mother. In other words, it was me that became my parent's first laboratory specimen in which their true patience developed.

All throughout my younger years there were probably many moments when my parents wondered how I'd make it through life. A common phrase my father used to help prep me for the day I left the nest was, "You're in for a rude awakening!" This was a statement that seemed to come out when I'd pushed his patience to the limit. I never liked hearing him utter that phrase, however, it was very successful in teaching me to be accountable with my attitude and actions.

Of all of the teachable moments of patience my parents endured there's one that really stands out for me. I was sixteen years old and it was a bitter cold night in February. I'd only been driving with a license for five months and didn't have experience with all the snow and ice which now covered the roads. Young drivers mixed with snow and ice can be a very dangerous combination on the road, but also in driveways.

I was dating a girl from my class at the time. We'd spent the evening at our house and I was preparing to take her home. We'd carefully made our way across the icy pavement to the old 1979 Ford Pinto waiting just outside of the garage. As we closed the car doors I had no idea how quickly an enjoyable evening would turn into one of my most embarrassing moments in my life.

The Pinto was stick shift and required the use of a clutch to change gears. I'd placed my left foot onto the clutch and slowly depressed it to start the car. I began to turn the ignition and at that precise moment felt my left foot slip from the clutch causing the car to lurch forward. Now in most situations this wouldn't have been an issue, but in this particular situation the garage door happened to get in the way. The Pinto slammed into the door with amazing force. My jaw dropped in total shock of what had transpired while my very supportive girlfriend literally burst into laughter at me.

After a few brief seconds of sitting in utter disbelief my parents came rushing to the scene. My father was the first to the car with a look of total bewilderment across his face. "What did you do!?" were his first words which were quickly followed by, "It sounded like a bomb went off out here. The whole house was shaking!" As each word continued to spew from his mouth I could feel my face turning another shade of red. Thank goodness it was dark outside and went unnoticed by my date who continued to sit and giggle. After a short while the excitement died down. I carefully pulled the car out of the garage door and proceeded to take my date home.

When I returned home, there wasn't very much said about the newly reshaped garage door. In fact, I can't remember much discussion with my parents at all. More than likely they'd realized it was an accident and there was nothing more needed to be said. I also believe it was due to the abundance of patience they'd developed through my first fifteen years under their roof. Their patience, gained over the years, allowed them to handle the situation with understanding and grace.

Moments with God

"Be completely humble and gentle; be patient bearing with one another in love." –Ephesians 4:2

It's hard to fathom the patience of God. With the abundance of sin and corruption taking place throughout our world it's hard to imagine how God could continue to care. People continue to turn their back on His love and grace yet He patiently waits to give of Himself to those who repent and turn from their sin.

In my forty-two years of life, I've been fortunate to have heard and read many wonderful teachings about God. I've seen God's patience with man resonate throughout the Bible. There are countless stories of people who turned their back and openly denied knowing of Him. The amazing thing about these stories is how God patiently waited for them to come to their senses. It took longer for some, but God's continued presence was the life changing element allowing them to become whole again.

In the book of James, it's discussed how believers must learn to plant patience into their lives and let it grow. Planting patience while believing and waiting for God to answer can take a load of self-control and trust in Him. Many people in the Bible waited for weeks, months, and even years for God's answer. Could it be that God's timing was an effort on His part to teach the same patience He had to endure for their sins?

The God that was ever present and patient in the Bible is the same God who patiently waits for us today. We also must learn to plant and cultivate the patience of Abraham and Moses. To become patient, as God is patient, should be considered one of the greatest goals we could achieve in life.

When I'd first received word about my father's cancer patience was the last thing on my mind. To endure the long journey before his surgery, our family learned firsthand the importance of patience. Upon planting this patience over the three months leading to the surgery we needed trust and belief for God to see us through. This trust and belief became the water and sun which allowed our patience to continue to grow.

Whatever road we find ourselves on or circumstances we face, we must learn to calmly continue to be patient for God. God works with a divine timeline, one based on His will in our lives. Knowing this, the final ultimate choice falls directly onto our laps. We can remain ever fearful and anxious about our difficulties, or place them at the foot of the cross and patiently wait on the Lord.

God's word states that if we earnestly seek the Lord we'll surely find Him. When we have complete faith and trust in Him our lives will be changed forever. He's our shelter in the storm and guiding light of comfort. He stands firmly by our side upholding us through it all.

As I reflect one last time upon the patience of my parents, it's become even clearer that their patience was truly a reflection of God's patience. Not everyone will experience having a child running a car through a garage door, but there will be many other unique opportunities to plant and grow patience with others. We need only to be aware of these moments and seize them as they arise.

Prayer

Dear God, help me to become a reflection of Your patience. When difficult situations arise in my daily life, may I be a living example of Your patience. For You are the Lord, You are the most high, the giver of all good things. I praise Your name today and all days. Thank You for Your patience with me in my life. Thank You for accepting me as Your own. Amen.

CHAPTER 18

Love

Chapter 18
Love

I consider this the best of the "Big 3." Between faithfulness, patience, and love, love definitely rises above the others. The word love describes why God created us. Without love, life would be completely miserable. I witnessed God's love for me profoundly through my battle with cancer. From different prayer blankets I'd received, the cards and notes, along with all of the well wishes through phone calls and prayers offered up for me. I was especially touched by the love of my family. God was truly present in each one of them.

-Jim

The most basic fabric of any person, family, city, and country is a word called love. Love is essential to all facets of life regardless of age, race, or culture. Love unifies and binds everything that matters in life. Without love the world would cease to exist.

I was very fortunate to have grown up in a home full of love. My parents expressed love through sacrifice, discipline, hard work, and their dedication to our family. These actions combined with their affection for each other produced an unshakeable foundation. Our family shared its ups and downs like most others, but never once did I question my parents love for me.

One of the greatest ways my parents expressed this love was through an endless support with everything I'd become involved with.

Actually, I could probably write an entire book on the thousands of events they'd taken part in supporting through the years. It wasn't always a verbal "I love you," but their expression of love through support was just as priceless.

One of my fondest memories of love through support was when my mother decided to enter college and pursue a degree in nursing. Those who have gone back to school as adults can certainly relate to the many sacrifices made during that time. When a family is part of this equation it takes a large effort from everyone in the household, especially the spouse.

When I reflect back upon those days, I've become much more appreciative of everything that transpired. My father had a fulltime job and did everything in his power to keep up with our daily needs. He cooked, cleaned, did laundry, saw us off to school, along with many other countless things around the house. We did our best to help out, but he was the difference maker. Everything he did helped to lighten the load for my mother which enabled her to focus on her studies. She went on to do very well in school and graduate the nursing program with honors.

The neat thing about this story is, I've had the opportunity to see the same process repeated with my two sisters. I truly believe the success they saw when our mother went back to school made a difference in their decision to go down a similar path. My sister Angie graduated from the same nursing program my mother had attended while my other sister Jennifer is currently in a radiology technology program. Both of them have children and two wonderful husbands who have displayed the same love and support I witnessed from my father. I'm very proud of all of them.

A couple of years ago I released a children's book titled "Bryanna and the Sand." It was inspired by and dedicated to my own daughter Bryanna whom the illustrator, Phyllis Stewart, portrayed so wonderfully in the book. The story is about a father and daughter who embark for a walk along the beach. During the expedition he teaches her a valuable lesson about love through the use of a simple handful of sand. The following is an excerpt from the book:

Bryanna's father sat down on the beach, picked up a handful of sand, and let it slowly slip between his fingers.

Bryanna sat beside him and watched as the sand landed gently on the beach.

"Listen to it, Bryanna. Can you hear it?"

Bryanna leaned closer to her father's hand but she couldn't hear anything because of the waves splashing in the distance. Then he told her, "Pick up some sand and feel it in your hands."

Bryanna picked up a handful of sand, "It feels so soft."

"And how does it look?"

"It looks like millions of diamonds sparkling in the sun."

Her father put him arm around her and pulled her close to him. "Bryanna, love is very much like the sand you are holding."

"What do you mean?"

"Just like the sand that you couldn't hear falling from my fingers, love is something we can't always hear. But just as we felt the softness of the sand in our hands and between our toes, we can feel love."

Bryanna smiled.

"Probably the most wonderful thing about love is that we can see it. Love is as beautiful as the sand sparkling like millions of diamonds. We see it in a hug or kiss and in many other special ways people openly care for one another."

"But where does love come from Daddy?"

"Love comes from deep in your heart. It's something very special and meant to be shared. And just as a flower blooms, love sits in our hearts waiting for its chance to bloom. When it does, it's as beautiful as any flower you will ever see."

It was truly a joy putting this book together. My main focus was to create a special way for children to visualize the magnificent beauty of love. What better way than to utilize a piece of nature God has so richly blessed us with. Being able to capture a magical teaching moment between a father and daughter only added to what I was attempting to achieve.

Having been on two separate cancer journeys with both of my parents I've also learned how important the bond of love is in difficult times. The unshakable foundation created through years of love between each other was able to hold firm against the storms. My siblings and I were able to use the same love and support we'd received through the years and reflect it directly back to our parents. We were simply living out the wonderful example of love we'd been so fortunate to be taught.

The discussion around love in my family would be infinite. I've been very blessed. My parents are both true inspirations who've demonstrated love in many ways and continue to do so. My wife and I have children who are blessed with not one, but two sets of grandparents that are exceptional examples of love.

Moments with God

*"For God so loved the world that he gave his one and only Son,
that whoever believes in him shall not perish but have eternal life."*

-John 3:16

There isn't a more powerful verse in scripture than John 3:16. The foundation of Christianity is laid out before us in one powerful sentence. Without God's love He wouldn't have given His one and only Son. Without God's love we wouldn't have had the opportunity to believe in this Son, or the opportunity to experience eternal life. Without God's love we wouldn't exist.

John 3:16 has several key points of interest. First, is the statement of God's love for the world. His love is unconditional with no boundaries. Regardless of how awful we've sinned or run from God he continues to love us the same.

Second, it's through this unconditional love that God sent His Son Jesus to conquer sin once and for all. It's hard enough to imagine sacrificing your own life to save a friend, but to have your own child become a sacrifice is difficult to comprehend. The mere fact Jesus lived on earth and died for our benefit is a very difficult thing to grasp, yet it's the most important concept of Christianity. When Jesus carried the cross to Calvary He was carrying and conquering the sins of the world so we might be saved and gain eternal life in heaven.

We do, however, have a responsibility in the light of such a great sacrifice. This brings us to the final point of John 3:16. In order to be forgiven and gain eternal life we must first believe in Jesus. We must believe that through His death Jesus paid the full price for our sins, and through His resurrection we've been washed clean and gain entrance into paradise for eternal life. We need only to repent and believe. How awesome is that!?

Where are you on your journey today? Are you rolling right along believing and serving God faithfully, or have you become too busy in your daily life and slipped away from Him? It's important to know God's always been in the business of second chances, examples can be found throughout the Bible. He stands willing and waiting with His arms open wide.

If this book has touched you in a special way, and I truly hope it has, it's my humble prayer you'll believe in Jesus and accept Him as the Lord of your life and Savior. You can search high and low for years on end to fill the emptiness in your heart that only God can fill. I urge you to turn to Him now, don't wait another day!

Prayer

(To accept or reaffirm your relationship with Jesus)

Dear Father, I know I've wandered but I've come home. Please accept me as Your son/daughter. I have chosen to turn from my sin. I place all of my faith and trust in Your Son, Jesus Christ, alone. I receive Him as my Savior and Lord. I want to only serve and follow You. Please give me the wisdom and strength I will need to avoid falling from You. I pray that today will be a new beginning to my journey as a member of Your family. Amen.

Final Thoughts

(June 7, 2010, North Topsail Island, North Carolina)

There's nothing quite like standing on a beach listening to the sound of the surf breaking. It has a unique way of creeping into the depths of ones soul and bathing it with a sense of tranquility.

I stepped into the warm water and felt the waves lapping at my feet as they sank into the wet sand. With one fluid motion I tossed the line and bait into the depths of the pounding surf. As I reeled my line taught I paused for a moment to glance at my father. In an instant my thoughts drifted off to his miraculous journey 2 years ago before watching him cast in his own line. I just shook my head and smiled.

I'll never fully comprehend the will of God or why He chose to perform such a miracle for my father, but it will resonate within me forever. To be on the receiving end of God's messages of comfort and love through Isaiah 41:10 was inspirational and awesome!

The journey has become a ministry for my father. His story has served as a beacon of hope for those who are hurting, and a living testimony to God's miraculous ways.

Two years ago I thought I'd never have the opportunity to fish the surf again with my father. To be standing on the beach with him was almost surreal. I took another glance to convince myself he was truly there before smiling and looking heavenward, whispering, "Thank You God, thank You."

The Yosick Family 2009

About the Authors

Jeff is the author of seven children's books. His mission is to write stories which contain valuable life lessons everyone can learn from, both young and old. Jeff's efforts to produce meaningful and heartfelt stories were rewarded when he was presented with the Cal writer's award for his book "Timmy and the Storm" in 2008.

Although Jeff considers writing to be a wonderful thing, his visits to schools and other organizations to share his stories are his favorite part of being an author. "If I can produce a story that will have an impact or make a difference in at least one person's life, then I've accomplished what I've set out to do. Having the opportunity to share my work and see in person how they touch people's lives makes writing that much more rewarding."

Jeff enjoys traveling and considers anywhere near an ocean his second home. He resides in Blacklick, Ohio, with his wife Valerie and three children.

This is Jim's first venture in writing. He considers the miraculous events of 2008 as not only an opportunity, but a calling to minister to others. His message of hope found in God through difficult times not only rings true through this book, but is witnessed everywhere he speaks.

Jim and his wife Barb reside in New Washington, Ohio, and are both retired. They've been married for 44 years and consider each day spent together a new blessing. Their greatest joy in life is found through time spent with their children and grandchildren.

To schedule the authors for a speaking engagement or book signing at your church or other organization, feel free to contact Jeff or Jim by phone or email. They welcome each opportunity to share this story and look forward to hearing from you.

jeff@jyosick.com or jyosick2@yahoo.com
Phone: 614-634-0378
Website: www.jyosick.com